MY BIG

QUESTION
and
ANSWER
BOOK

KINGfISHER

KINGFISHER
Kingfisher Publications Plc
New Penderel House
283–288 High Holborn
London WC1V 7HZ

First published by Kingfisher Publications Plc in 2000
Material in this edition previously published in four separate
volumes as part of the *Questions and Answers* series
10 9 8 7 6 5 4 3 2 1

1TR(PB)/BS/0700/TWP/150SMA

A CIP catalogue for this book is available from the British Library.

ISBN 0 7534 0563 6 (hb)
ISBN 0 7534 0564 4 (pb)

Printed in Singapore

Authors: Robin Kerrod, Wendy Madgwick
Designed, edited and typeset: Tucker Slingsby Ltd

Illustrations:
Jonathan Adams, Susanna Addario, Marion Appleton, Julian Baker, Sue Barclay, Owain Bell,
Gary Bines, Simone Boni, Richard Bonson, Peter Bull, John Burgess, Vanessa Card, Robin Carter,
Jim Channel, Kuo Kang Chen, Stephen Conlin, Peter Dennis, Francesca D'Ottavi, Sandra Doyle,
Richard Draper, Angelika Elsebach, James Field, Chris Forsey, Terry Gabbey, Luigi Galante, Lee
Gibbons, Peter Goodfellow, Jeremy Gower, Ruby Green, Peter Gregory, Ray Grinaway, Alan
Hardcastle, Donald Harley, Nick Harris, Tim Hayward, Nicholas Hewitson, Adam Hook, Christian
Hook, Biz Hull, David Hurrel, Mark Iley, Ian Jackson, Roger Kent, Terence Lambert, Ruth Lindsay,
Bernard Long, Chris Lyons, Kevin Maddison, Shirley Mallinson, Janos Marffy, Josephine Martin, John
Marshall, David McAllister, Angus McBride, Robert Morton, William Oliver, Nicki Palin, Alex Pang, Roger Payne,
Mark Pepe, Melvyn Pickering, Sebastian Quigley, Andrew Robinson, Bernard Robinson, Eric Robson, Michael Roffe,
Mike Saunders, Nick Shrewring, Tim Slade, Guy Smith, Tony Smith, Mark Stacey, Roger Stewart, George Thompson,
Ian Thompson, Rose Walton, Wendy Webb, Andrea Wheatcroft, Sohraya Willis, Ann Winterbotham, David Wright

Picture credits:
p. 5 and p. 120 cr Nokia; p. 54 tl courtesy of the Department Library Services, American Museum of Natural
History, Neg. no. 410 764, Shackleford 1925; p. 123 br Science Photo Library; p. 125 c Science Photo
Library/Mehau Kulyk; p. 145 cl Nokia; p. 147 bl Mary Evans Picture Library

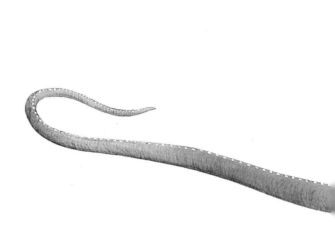

Contents

Contents

ANCIENT CIVILIZATIONS

Contents

STARS AND
PLANETS

Looking at the Sky

The night sky is one of the most beautiful sights in nature. Stars beyond number shine out of a velvety blackness, bright planets wander among the stars and long-tailed comets come and go. Astronomy, the study of the night sky, is one of the most ancient sciences.

What can we see?

Although we can see a lot in the night sky with just our eyes, we can see much more through binoculars or telescopes. To the naked eye the Moon looks small, and we see few features. With binoculars and telescopes it looks larger, and we can see craters on its surface.

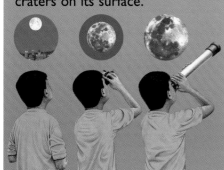

Who invented telescopes?

A Dutchman named Hans Lippershey built the first telescope in 1608. But it was Galileo, an Italian, who first used one to study the night sky. He made his first observations in the winter of 1609–10. He spied the moons of Jupiter, craters on Earth's Moon and spots on the Sun. Galileo's telescope was quite small. Later devices, known as 'aerial' telescopes, were around 50 metres long.

When did people first start studying the stars?

People must have been star-gazing for millions of years. But they probably began studying the night sky seriously only about 5,000 years ago. Early civilizations in the Middle East left records of their observations. The Babylonians were skilled observers, and we know the Egyptians were too, because they lined up their pyramids with certain constellations, or star patterns. In Britain, around 2800 BC, Stonehenge was built, possibly as a kind of observatory. Stones were lined up to show the positions of the Sun and Moon at different seasons. Ancient Chinese and Mayan astronomers left accurate records of their observations.

Stonehenge

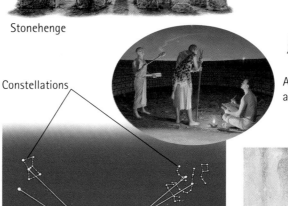

Constellations

Shafts   Pyramid

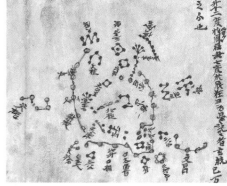

Mayan astronomer

Ancient Egyptian astronomer-priests

Ancient Chinese star map

Aerial telescope

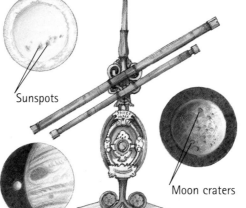

Sunspots

Moon craters

Jupiter   Galileo's telescope

How do radio telescopes work?

Stars give off radio waves as well as light waves. Astronomers have built telescopes to pick up these radio waves. Radio telescopes are not like light telescopes. Most are huge metal dishes, which can be tilted and turned to any part of the sky. The dishes pick up radio waves, or signals, and focus them onto an aerial. The signals are sent to a receiver and then to a computer, which changes them into images.

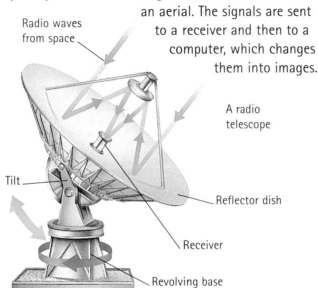

Radio waves from space

Tilt

Reflector dish

Receiver

Revolving base

A radio telescope

Quick-fire Quiz

1. What's the study of stars called?
a) Astronautics
b) Astronomy
c) Aerobics

2. Who first studied the stars using a telescope?
a) The ancient Britons
b) The Mayans
c) Galileo

3. How long were some of the early 'aerial' telescopes?
a) 5m
b) 50m
c) 150m

4. Where are modern observatories built?
a) On the Moon
b) On mountains
c) In valleys

Where do astronomers work?

Astronomers look at, or observe, the stars from observatories. The great domes on these observatories house big telescopes which use curved mirrors to collect the light from the stars. Some mirrors are as big as 10 metres across. Modern-day astronomers do not often look through these telescopes. Instead they use them as giant cameras and take pictures with them. Most observatories today are built on mountains, above the thickest part of the atmosphere, where the air is cleaner and clearer.

What is special about space telescopes?

Some of the outstanding discoveries of recent years have been made by space telescopes. Out in space, telescopes can get a much clearer view of the night sky than they can from Earth. Also, space telescopes can pick up invisible rays, such as X-rays, which cannot pass through the atmosphere.

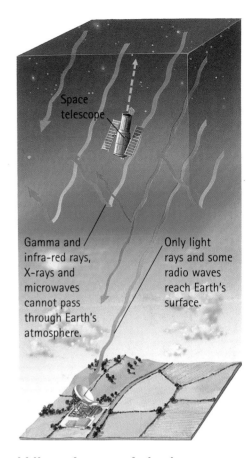

Space telescope

Gamma and infra-red rays, X-rays and microwaves cannot pass through Earth's atmosphere.

Only light rays and some radio waves reach Earth's surface.

Seeing Stars

Using just your eyes, you can see thousands of stars in the night sky. If you look closely, you will see that some are brighter than others. The bright stars make patterns that you can recognize every time you go star-gazing. We call them constellations.

Northern hemisphere

Plough

Celestial sphere

Earth's axis

Plane of equator

Equator

Plane of eclipse (path of the Sun)

Southern hemisphere

Southern Cross

Can we all see the same stars?

Because Earth is round and just rotates on its north-south axis, we only see the stars above the hemisphere in which we live. Earth seems to be in the middle of a great dark ball, which we call the celestial sphere. People in the far north can always see the Plough but never the Southern Cross, which is seen in the far south. In the far south, no-one ever sees the Plough. People near the Equator can see almost all the stars at some time of the year.

The signs of the Zodiac

What are star signs?

During the year, the Sun appears to move through the stars of the celestial sphere. It seems to pass through 12 main constellations, called the constellations of the Zodiac. They are also called star signs, and are important in astrology. Astrologers believe that human lives are affected by the stars.

Leo the Lion   Scorpio the Scorpion

The night sky in the
Southern hemisphere

Some of the major constellations

Northern hemisphere	Southern hemisphere
1. Pegasus	1. Aquarius (The Water-bearer)
2. Perseus	2. Orion (The Hunter)
3. Pole Star	3. Scorpio (The Scorpion)
4. Plough (or Little Bear)	4. Southern Cross
5. Great Bear	5. Hydra (Water Snake)
6. Leo (The Lion)	6. Libra (Scales)

Why do the stars move across the sky?

If you go out star-gazing at night, you will notice that the constellations gradually move across the sky from east to west, as the Sun does during the day. Ancient astronomers thought that the stars were fixed on the inside of the celestial sphere, and that this sphere was spinning round Earth, which stood still. We now know that the opposite is true. It is Earth that is moving and the stars that are standing still. Earth spins round in space, moving from west to east. This makes the stars appear to travel in the opposite direction.

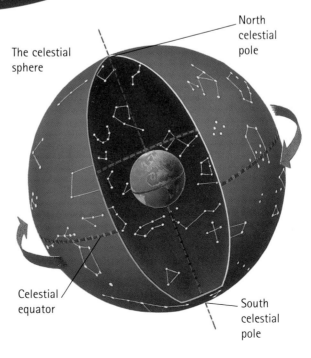

The celestial sphere

North celestial pole

Celestial equator

South celestial pole

Quick-fire Quiz

1. What's a pattern of bright stars called?
a) Congregation
b) Constellation
c) Configuration

2. From where can you see the Plough?
a) Everywhere
b) The south
c) The north

3. Which way do the stars seem to travel overhead?
a) North to south
b) East to west
c) West to east

4. How many star signs are there?
a) 10
b) 12
c) 20

Great Balls of Gas

Stars look like tiny bright specks in the night sky. But they are not tiny at all. They are in fact huge balls of searing hot gas. Stars look small only because they lie many million, million kilometres away. If you could get close to a star, you would find that it looked like our Sun, because the Sun is a star too.

Do stars last forever?

Just like living things, stars are born, grow older and, in time, die. The pictures below show two different ways in which stars die. After shining steadily for some time the stars swell up into a red giant. Some red giants shrink into a white, then a black dwarf. This will happen to the Sun one day. Other stars swell up from a red giant to a supergiant before exploding as a supernova.

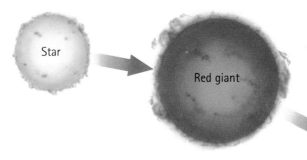

Star

Red giant

Outer layers break away

Supergiant

Quick-fire Quiz

1. What is an exploding star called?
a) Supergiant
b) Supernova
c) Superstar

2. What will our Sun be one day?
a) A supernova
b) A black dwarf
c) A black hole

3. Which is the hottest?
a) Sun
b) Red giant
c) Blue-white star

4. Which is the smallest?
a) Sun
b) Supergiant
c) Pulsar

How big are stars?

We can measure the size of one star directly because it is so close. This is our own star, the Sun. The Sun measures nearly 1,400,000 kilometres across. Astronomers can work out the size of other stars too. They have discovered that there are many stars smaller than the Sun, and also many much larger. Astronomers call the Sun a dwarf star. They know of red giant stars tens of times bigger, and supergiant stars tens of times bigger still. Some supergiants measure 400 million kilometres across.

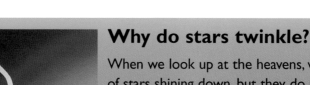

Why do stars twinkle?

When we look up at the heavens, we can see thousands of stars shining down, but they do not give out a steady light. They seem to twinkle, or change brightness all the time. In fact they do shine steadily but air currents in the Earth's atmosphere make the starlight bend this way and that. Some of the light gets into our eyes and some is bent away. So, to us on Earth, the stars seem to twinkle.

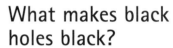

How hot are stars?

Stars are great globes of very hot gas, but their temperature varies quite a lot. Astronomers can tell the temperature of a star by the colour and brightness of the light it gives out. Yellowish stars like the Sun have a temperature of about 5,500°C. This compares with about 3,000°C for a dim red star to 30,000°C for a bright blue-white star.

White dwarf

Dead black dwarf

Why do some stars explode?

Massive stars explode when they come to the end of their lives. They swell up into huge supergiants. Supergiants are unstable, so they collapse and blast themselves to pieces in an explosion called a supernova. Supernovae are the biggest explosions in the Universe, as bright as billions of Suns put together.

Black hole

Supernova

Pulsar

What makes black holes black?

After a star explodes as a supernova, what is left of it shrinks rapidly. If it is really big, it shrinks almost to nothing. All that is left is a tiny region of space that has enormous gravity. The gravity is so great that the tiny region will suck in all nearby matter, including other stars. The name 'black hole' comes from the fact that the pull it exerts is so powerful that even light cannot escape from it.

What is a pulsar?

A smaller star that explodes as a supernova ends its life as a tiny star we call a pulsar. It gets this name because it 'pulsates', or sends out pulses of energy. Astronomers think that pulsars spin round fast and send out narrow beams of energy. On Earth we see a pulse of energy when this beam sweeps past us.

A pulsar passing Earth

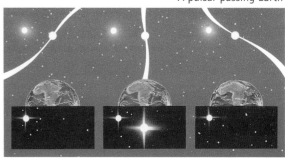

13

Galaxies

From Earth, space seems to be full of stars. But if you travelled a long way from Earth, you would in time leave the stars behind. Looking back, you would see that the stars form a kind of island in space. In other directions, you would see other star islands, which we call galaxies. The galaxies and the space they occupy make up the Universe.

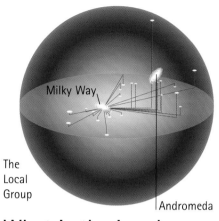

What is the Local Group of galaxies?

There are thousands of galaxies in space. Many are in groups called clusters. The galaxy where we live is called the Milky Way, which is in a cluster we call the Local Group. The Milky Way is the second-largest galaxy in the Local Group. The largest is the Andromeda galaxy.

Do all galaxies look the same?

Astronomers can see galaxies of all shapes and sizes through their telescopes. Some are known as barred spiral galaxies. They have curved arms coming from a bar through their centre (1). Ordinary spirals do not have the bar. Elliptical galaxies (2) have an oval shape. Galaxies with no particular shape are called irregulars (3).

How do galaxies form?

Galaxies begin to form in clouds of dark gas so huge that even light would take hundreds of thousands of years to cross them. Over time, gravity begins to pull the particles of gas together. Gradually, the gas cloud shrinks and it becomes more and more dense. Here and there it becomes dense enough for stars to form. At the same time the gas cloud starts to rotate and flatten out.

1 A huge cloud of gas shrinks and becomes denser. Stars form in the centre.

2 The starry cloud spins, and flattens into a disc shape.

3 Matter in the disc collects on arms, where more stars form.

How did the Universe begin?

Astronomers believe that the Universe began with a huge explosion known as the Big Bang. They reckon it happened more than 15,000 million years ago. The Big Bang created a hot bubble of space that has been getting bigger and bigger ever since. Astronomers believe the Universe is constantly expanding.

Big Bang

The Universe expands after the Big Bang

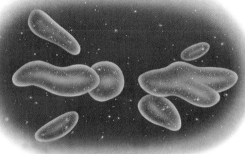

Superclusters

What makes up the Universe?

Simply speaking, the Universe is made up of matter and space. The matter is found as planets, moons and stars. The stars gather together into great galaxies, and the galaxies gather into groups, or clusters. Even the clusters gather together to form gigantic superclusters of galaxies. The Universe is made up of millions of these superclusters.

The Milky Way – a spiral galaxy

Quick-fire Quiz

1. What is the galaxy our Sun and its planets are in called?
a) The Heavens
b) The Milky Bar
c) The Milky Way

2. Which of these is brightest?
a) Star
b) Quasar
c) Galaxy

3. What began the Universe?
a) Gravity
b) Black holes
c) The Big Bang

4. Which of these is the Universe doing?
a) Expanding
b) Exploding
c) Shrinking

What are quasars?

Quasars look like stars. But they are so far away that, for us to detect them, they must be brighter than thousands of galaxies together. Astronomers think quasars get their great power from black holes. As matter is sucked into a black hole, enormous energy is given out as light and other radiation.

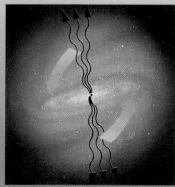

15

The Solar System

Every day, the Sun travels across the sky from east to west. It looks as if it circles Earth, but the opposite is true – Earth circles the Sun. Earth is part of the Sun's family, or Solar System. It is one of nine bodies called planets that circle the Sun.

Who first realized that Earth travels round the Sun?

Early astronomers thought the Sun and other planets circled the Earth. Nicolaus Copernicus (1473–1543) was a Polish priest and astronomer. He came up with the theory that the Sun was the centre of the Universe, and that Earth and the planets moved round it. This was the first real challenge to the idea that Earth was the centre of the Universe, which ancient astronomers believed. Copernicus published his theory while he lay dying in 1543, but religious leaders opposed his ideas for many years.

How big is the Solar System?

Earth is nearly 150 million kilometres from the Sun. This seems a huge distance, but it is only a small step in space. The furthest planets lie thousands of millions of kilometres away from the Sun. The diagram on the right shows the orbits, or paths, of the nine planets round the Sun. The distance from one side of Pluto's orbit to the other is nearly 15,000 million kilometres.

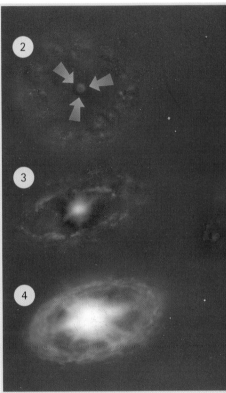

What happened at the birth of the Solar System?

1 The Solar System was born in a great cloud of gas and dust about 5,000 million years ago. There are many clouds like this, called nebulae, in the space between the stars.

The orbits of the planets around the Sun

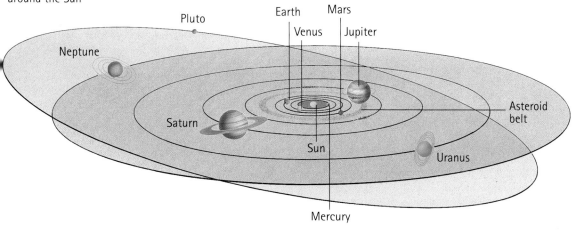

Pluto
Neptune
Earth Mars
Venus Jupiter
Saturn
Asteroid belt
Sun
Uranus
Mercury

2 Some parts of the cloud became much denser. Gas and dust in these areas started to stick together under the pull of their gravity. In time they formed into a ball-shaped mass.

3 The ball shrank and warmed up. Slowly, it started to glow, forming a 'baby' Sun by the time it was about 100,000 years old.

4 The baby Sun was spinning rapidly, flinging off masses of material into space. All the while it was shrinking and getting hotter and hotter.

5 In time, the baby Sun became hot enough to set off nuclear reactions. These produced the fantastic energy it needed to shine as a 'grown-up' star.

6 The ring of material thrown out earlier by the Sun began to clump together. It gradually formed larger and larger lumps at different distances from the Sun.

7 The large lumps grew into the planets we find today. Smaller lumps formed the moons of the planets, and even smaller lumps formed the asteroids.

17

Our Star, the Sun

The Sun is our local star. Like the other stars, it is a ball of very hot gas. It lies about 150 million kilometres from Earth, and is about 1.4 million kilometres across. The Sun pours huge amounts of energy into space. The light and heat that reach Earth make life possible.

Where does the Sun get its energy?

The energy that keeps the Sun shining is produced in its centre, or core. The pressure in the core is enormous, and the temperature reaches 15 million °C. Under these conditions, atoms of hydrogen gas fuse (join together) to form another gas, helium. This process is called nuclear fusion. It produces enormous amounts of energy.

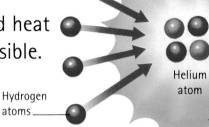

Hydrogen atoms

Helium atom

Energy

What is the Sun's surface like?

The Sun's surface is a bubbling, boiling mass of very hot gas, constantly in motion, like a stormy sea. Here and there, fountains of flaming gas thousands of kilometres high shoot out. These are called prominences. Eventually, they curve over and fall back. Violent explosions called flares also often take place, blasting particles into space that can cause magnetic storms on Earth.

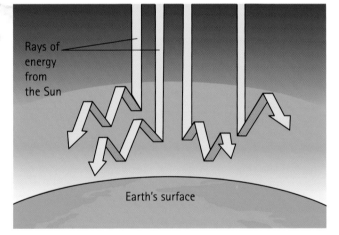

Rays of energy from the Sun

Earth's surface

What happens when the Sun warms Earth?

The Sun pours energy on to Earth, warming the land and the water in the oceans. Gases in the air trap the heat and warm the atmosphere. They act like a greenhouse, so the warming process is called the 'greenhouse effect'. One of the main gases that traps heat is carbon dioxide, produced when fuels burn.

Quick-fire Quiz

1. What is an explosion on the Sun called?
a) Prominence
b) Flare
c) Sunspot

2. What produces the Sun's energy?
a) Burning coal
b) Burning hydrogen
c) Nuclear fusion

3. Which gas in air traps heat?
a) Nitrogen
b) Carbon dioxide
c) Oxygen

4. How many more years will the Sun last?
a) 50 million
b) 500 million
c) 5,000 million

Is it safe to look at the Sun?

Never look directly at the Sun. Its light is so bright that it will damage your eyes and can even blind you. Instead, use binoculars or a telescope to throw an image onto paper, and look at that.

What is the Sun like inside?

The Sun is made up of a number of layers. In the centre is the very hot core, where energy is produced. This energy travels outwards by radiation, reaching the outer layer, called the convection region. There, currents of hot gas carry the energy to the surface (photosphere), where it escapes as light and heat. The temperature of the surface is about 5,500°C. Sunspots are dark patches on the surface. They are about 1,000°C cooler. Some sunspots grow to be bigger than Earth.

How do eclipses happen?

Occasionally, the Moon moves across the face of the Sun during the day, blotting out its light and casting a dark shadow on Earth. Day turns suddenly into night. We call this a total eclipse of the Sun. Eclipses occur because, from Earth, the Moon seems to be almost the same size as the Sun and can cover it up. Total eclipses can only be seen over a small part of Earth because the Moon casts only a small shadow.

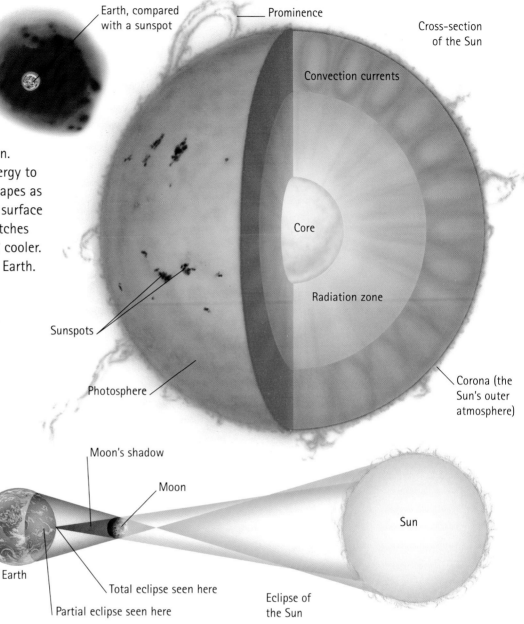

Earth, compared with a sunspot

Prominence

Cross-section of the Sun

Convection currents

Core

Radiation zone

Sunspots

Photosphere

Corona (the Sun's outer atmosphere)

Moon's shadow

Moon

Earth

Total eclipse seen here

Partial eclipse seen here

Sun

Eclipse of the Sun

Will the Sun always shine?

1 The Sun was born, along with the rest of the Solar System, about 5,000 million years ago. It has been shining steadily ever since.

2 In another 5,000 million years' time, the Sun will swell up and get hotter. Earth's oceans will boil away and all life will die.

3 As the Sun gets bigger and hotter and redder, Earth will be scorched to a cinder. In time it may be swallowed by the Sun's outer layers.

4 Gradually, the red giant Sun will begin to shrink again. Eventually it will become a white dwarf star about the size of Earth.

The Planets

Jupiter

The nine planets are the most important members of the Sun's family. In order of distance from the Sun, they are Mercury, Venus, Earth, Mars, Jupiter, Saturn, Uranus, Neptune and Pluto. The first four are small rocky bodies. The next four are giants, made up mainly of gas. Pluto is a tiny ball of rock and ice.

Mercury

Venus

Earth

Mars

How big are the planets?

The pictures on these two pages show the relative sizes of the planets. You might think that Earth is a big place. But look how much bigger some of the other planets are! Even the biggest planets, however, are dwarfed by the Sun. The Sun is nearly ten times bigger across than Jupiter, and it could swallow more than a million Earths. However, Earth is bigger than four of the planets – nearby Venus, Mars and Mercury, and tiny, distant Pluto.

Sun

Which is the biggest planet?

Jupiter is by far the largest of the planets. It has more mass than all the other planets put together. It measures nearly 143,000 kilometres across, which is 11 times bigger than Earth. Even though it is so big, it takes less than 10 hours for it to spin round once. This means that its surface is spinning round at a speed of 45,000 kilometres an hour. This is 30 times faster than Earth spins.

Which planets have rings?

Once it was thought that Saturn was the only planet that had rings around it because they were the only ones that can be seen through a telescope. But close-up photographs taken by the *Voyager* space probes have shown us that the other three gas giants – Jupiter, Uranus and Neptune – have rings too. The rings around these other planets are much thinner, narrower and darker than Saturn's.

Why is Uranus sometimes called 'new'?

Astronomers have been studying the planets for thousands of years. They have watched the way they move, or 'wander', across the night sky, unlike the stars. But the ancient astronomers could only see five planets in the night sky. It was not until 1781 that someone built a telescope powerful enough to spot another planet, which came to be called Uranus. Uranus was the first of three 'new' planets to be discovered. Neptune was discovered in 1846, and Pluto in 1930.

Uranus

Quick-fire Quiz

1. Which of these has rings?
a) Pluto
b) Saturn
c) Venus

2. How many planets are bigger than Earth?
a) Two
b) Three
c) Four

3. How fast does Jupiter spin?
a) 4,500 km/h
b) 45,000 km/h
c) 450,000 km/h

4. When was the last planet discovered?
a) 1781
b) 1930
c) 1979

What is special about Saturn?

Two things are outstanding about Saturn. One is obvious when you look at the planet through a telescope. The planet is surrounded by a set of bright, shining rings. Many people think that these make Saturn the most beautiful object in the Solar System. The other special thing about Saturn is that it is the lightest (least dense) of all the planets. It is lighter even than water. This means that if you could place it in a huge bowl of water, it would float.

Rings

Saturn

Which planet is furthest from the Sun?

As far as we know, the most distant planet from the Sun is Pluto, the last 'new' planet to be discovered after Neptune. But Pluto is not always the furthest away. For 20 years between 1979 and 1999, Neptune was further still because during this time Pluto was travelling inside Neptune's orbit. Neptune will become the furthest planet again in a little over 200 years' time. Pluto travels more than 7,000 million kilometres away from the Sun. It takes nearly 248 Earth-years to circle the Sun once.

Pluto

Neptune

Mercury

Mercury is the planet closest to the Sun. It is also the fastest-moving planet, whizzing round the Sun in just 88 days. Being close to the Sun, Mercury gets extremely hot. Its surface is covered in thousands of craters, making it look rather like the Moon.

Mercury

Earth

How big is Mercury?

Mercury is the smallest of the rocky, Earth-like planets. With a diameter of only 4,880 kilometres, it is less than half the size of the Earth. The planet Pluto, a deep-frozen ball of rock and ice, is even smaller.

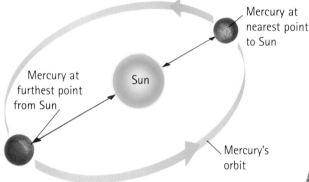

Mercury at nearest point to Sun

Mercury at furthest point from Sun

Sun

Mercury's orbit

What is strange about Mercury's orbit?

Most planets have a nearly circular orbit, or path, around the Sun. Mercury, however, has an oval orbit. At times it travels as far as 70 million kilometres away from the Sun. At others, it gets as close as 46 million kilometres.

Why does Mercury get so hot?

As it travels around the Sun, Mercury spins so slowly on its axis that a point on its surface stays in the Sun for nearly six Earth-months at a time. With the Sun so close and shining for so long, surface temperatures on Mercury soar to 430°C – hot enough to melt metals such as tin and lead.

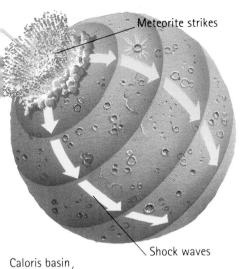

Meteorite strikes

Shock waves

Caloris basin

Craters

What has shaped Mercury's surface?

Billions of years ago, all the planets were bombarded by huge meteorites. On Earth, most craters made by the meteorites have been worn away by the action of the weather. Mercury has no weather because it has almost no atmosphere. So all the craters that formed ages ago remain, and the whole planet is covered with them. A huge one, called the Caloris Basin, was made by a giant meteorite that sent shock waves throughout the planet.

What is Mercury made of?

Like the Earth and the other rocky planets, Mercury is made up of different layers. Underneath a rocky crust there is a rocky mantle, and, at the centre, a huge metal core. The shrinking of the core has caused great ridges, up to 3 kilometres high, to appear on the surface.

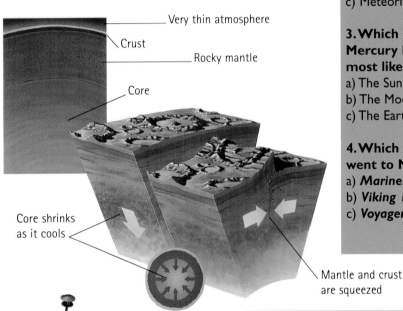

Very thin atmosphere

Crust

Rocky mantle

Core

Core shrinks as it cools

Mantle and crust are squeezed

Have any space probes visited Mercury?

Only one space probe has flown to study Mercury. Named *Mariner 10*, it flew to the planet in 1974, after visiting Venus. Its pictures revealed for the first time that Mercury looked rather like some parts of the Moon. *Mariner 10* flew past Mercury twice more. On the last occasion, in March 1975, it skimmed only about 300 kilometres above the surface.

Mariner 10

MERCURY DATA

Diameter at equator: *4,880km*
Mass: *0.06 times Earth's mass*
Average distance from Sun:
58 million km
Minimum distance from Earth:
91 million km
Length of day: *59 Earth-days*
Length of year: *88 Earth-days*
Temperature: *-185°C to 430°C*
Satellites: *0*

Venus

Venus is the planet whose orbit comes closest to Earth. We often see it shining in the western sky after sunset, which is why it is known as the Evening Star. Venus is a near twin of Earth in size, but it is a waterless world with a scorching climate.

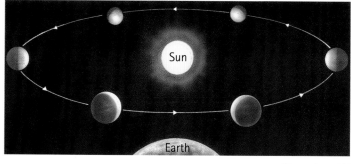

Venus in orbit

Why does Venus change shape?

From Earth, Venus seems to change its shape and size as time goes by. This is because it orbits closer to the Sun than Earth. When it is on the far side of the Sun, we see it as a small circle. As it moves closer to Earth, it gets bigger, but we only see it as a part-circle. Finally, it is just a thin crescent.

What is the surface of Venus like?

Space probes have shown that great plains cover much of Venus' surface. There are two big highland regions, which we can think of as continents. One is found in the north, and is called Ishtar Terra. The other lies near the equator, and is called Aphrodite Terra.

Venus landscape

Clouds cover the surface of Venus

Why is Venus so cloudy?

We cannot see Venus' surface from Earth because of thick clouds in its atmosphere. These clouds are not like the clouds we find on Earth, which are made up of tiny water droplets. Venus' clouds are made up of tiny droplets of sulphuric acid, one of the strongest acids we know. The sulphur has found its way into the atmosphere from the many volcanoes that have erupted on Venus over the years.

How can we see through Venus' clouds?

Space probes can see through Venus' clouds and show us what the planet's surface is like. But they do not 'see' in ordinary light. They 'see' with radar beams, because radar beams can go straight through clouds. The most successful radar probe, named *Magellan*, mapped the whole planet between 1990 and 1992.

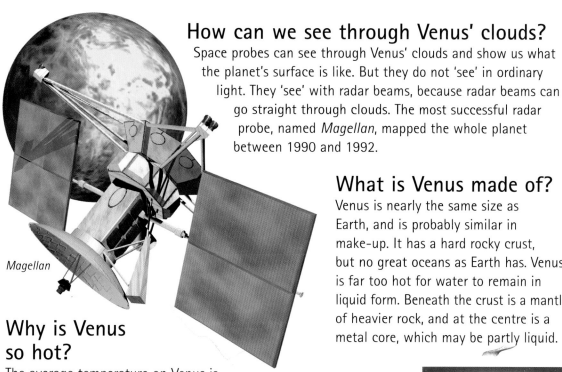

Magellan

What is Venus made of?

Venus is nearly the same size as Earth, and is probably similar in make-up. It has a hard rocky crust, but no great oceans as Earth has. Venus is far too hot for water to remain in liquid form. Beneath the crust is a mantle of heavier rock, and at the centre is a metal core, which may be partly liquid.

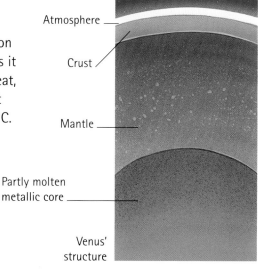

Atmosphere —

Crust —

Mantle —

Partly molten metallic core —

Venus' structure

Why is Venus so hot?

The average temperature on Venus is more than twice as hot as an oven set on 'high'. This is because its atmosphere contains mainly carbon dioxide – a heavy gas that traps heat. Over the years it has caused the atmosphere to trap more and more heat, as a greenhouse does. The cloud layers trap the heat too, making the temperature reach a scorching 480°C.

Venus' atmosphere

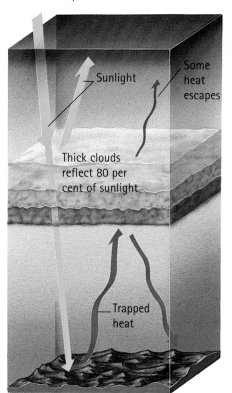

— Sunlight

Some heat escapes

Thick clouds reflect 80 per cent of sunlight

— Trapped heat

VENUS DATA

Diameter at equator: 12,100km
Average distance from Sun: 108 million km
Minimum distance from Earth: 42 million km
Turns on axis: 243 Earth-days
Circles Sun: 225 Earth-days
Surface temperature: 480°C
Satellites: 0

Earth

From space our home planet, Earth, appears to be mainly blue in colour. This is because of the colour of the oceans which cover over two-thirds of its surface. The land areas, or continents, cover less than a third. The layer of air above the surface is thin, but makes life on Earth possible.

Earth

What causes day and night?

Almost every place on Earth has a time when it is light (day), followed by a time when it is dark (night). Day and night come about because Earth spins round in space, and different parts of its surface face the Sun. It is daytime when a place is on the side of Earth facing the Sun. It becomes night when the place is on the side of Earth facing away from the Sun.

What makes Earth different?

A number of things make Earth different from the other planets. It is covered with great oceans of water, and its atmosphere contains lots of oxygen. The atmosphere also acts like a blanket, holding in enough of the Sun's heat to keep Earth at a comfortable temperature. The water, the oxygen and the temperature make Earth a suitable place for living things – at least one-and-a-half million different kinds of plants and animals.

Earth land and seascape

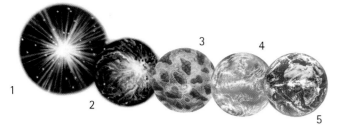

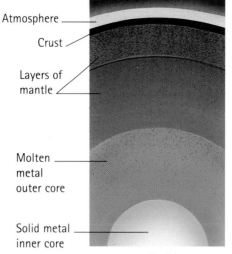

Earth's structure

How has Earth changed?

Earth formed about 4,600 million years ago when bits of matter in space came together (1). At first Earth was a great molten ball (2). It gradually cooled and the atmosphere and oceans eventually formed (3). In time, it changed into the world we know today (4 and 5), made up of layers of rock with a metal core. Our world is still changing. Currents in the rocks beneath the crust are widening the oceans, and driving the continents further apart (see below).

Atmosphere
Crust
Layers of mantle
Molten metal outer core
Solid metal inner core

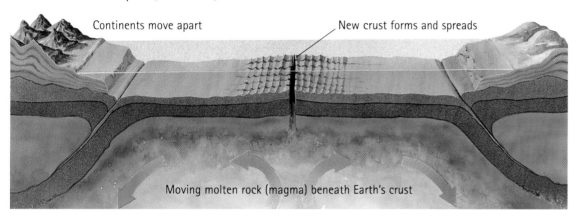

Continents move apart

New crust forms and spreads

Moving molten rock (magma) beneath Earth's crust

Over thousands of years, Earth's orbit changes from circular to elongated.

EARTH DATA

Diameter at equator: 12,756km
Average distance from Sun: 149.6 million km
Turns on axis: 23 hours 56 minutes
Year length: 365.25 days
Surface temperature: -89°C to 58°C
Satellites: 1 (the Moon)

What causes the seasons?

The changes in weather that we call the seasons happen because of the way Earth's axis is tilted in space. Because of this tilt, a place leans more towards the Sun and is warmer at some times of the year than at others. It is this that causes the changing seasons. The place tilted towards the Sun has summer, while the place leaning away has winter.

Spring
Northern summer
Northern winter
Autumn
21 March
21 December
Sun
21 June longest day in the north
23 September
Southern summer
Spring
Autumn
Southern winter

27

The Moon

Any object, or satellite, which orbits a planet is called a moon. Our Moon circles Earth once a month and is Earth's nearest neighbour in space. We can see it clearly through telescopes, and astronauts have explored it on foot. It is a small body – about a quarter the diameter of Earth. It has no atmosphere, no weather and no life.

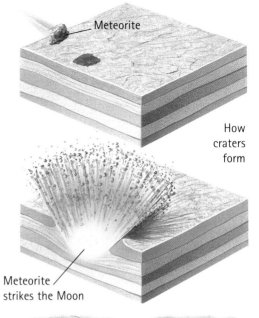

Meteorite

How craters form

Meteorite strikes the Moon

Terraced crater

Concentric crater

Ray crater

Ghost crater

How did the Moon form?

Most astronomers think that the Moon formed after another large body smashed into Earth thousand of millions of years ago (1). Material from Earth and the other body were flung into space. In time, this material came together to form the Moon (2). This explains why Moon rocks are different from rocks on Earth.

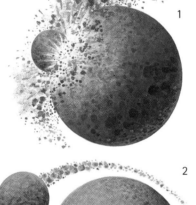

1

2

When did astronauts land on the Moon?

The first astronauts landed on the Moon on July 20, 1969. They were Edwin Aldrin and Neil Armstrong, the crew of the lunar landing module of the *Apollo 11* spacecraft. Armstrong was the first person to stand on the Moon. There were five more lunar landings – one more in 1969, two in 1971, and two in 1972.

Moon rock

What made the Moon's craters?

The surface of the Moon is covered with many thousands of pits, or craters. They have been made by meteorites raining down from outer space. Most large craters have stepped, or terraced, walls and mountain peaks in the middle. The largest craters are more than 200 kilometres across. Some young craters have bright streaks, or rays, coming from them, while only the tips of some old 'ghost' craters can be seen.

Where are the Moon's seas?

Early astronomers thought that the dark areas we see on the Moon might be seas. They called them 'maria', the Latin word for 'seas'. We know now that they are vast dusty plains, but we still call them seas. Most seas are found on the side of the Moon that always faces us, the near side. There are only one or two small seas on the opposite side, the far side.

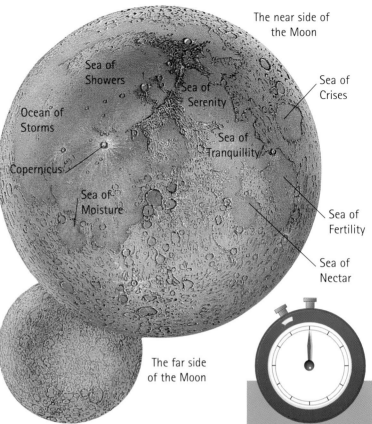

The near side of the Moon

Sea of Showers

Sea of Serenity

Ocean of Storms

Sea of Crises

Sea of Tranquillity

Copernicus

Sea of Moisture

Sea of Fertility

Sea of Nectar

The far side of the Moon

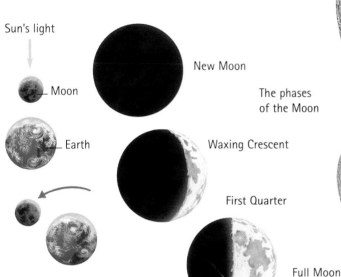

Sun's light

Moon

Earth

New Moon

The phases of the Moon

Waxing Crescent

First Quarter

Full Moon

Last Quarter

Waning Crescent

Why does the Moon change shape?

The Moon seems to change shape because we can only see the parts of it that are lit by the Sun. At New Moon, the unlit side faces Earth and it is invisible. Gradually, as the Moon circles Earth, we see more and more of the sunlit side, until Full Moon. Then we gradually see less and less, until it disappears. There are 29.5 days between one new moon and the next.

MOON DATA

Diameter at equator: *3,476km*
Minimum distance from Earth: *356,000km*
Time to circle Earth: *27.3 Earth-days*
Surface temperature: *-170°C to 110°C*

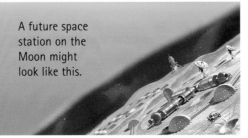

A future space station on the Moon might look like this.

Mars

Small and red in colour, Mars is more like Earth than any other planet. People once believed that intelligent beings lived on Mars – but space probes have shown that there are no Martians, and no other life on the planet. It is too cold, and the atmosphere is too thin for life to exist.

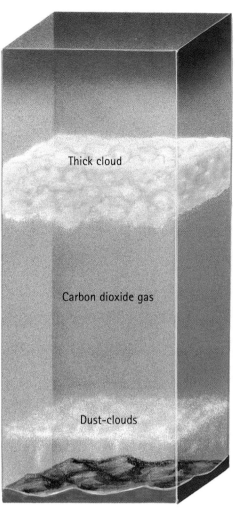

Mars' atmosphere

Thick cloud

Carbon dioxide gas

Dust-clouds

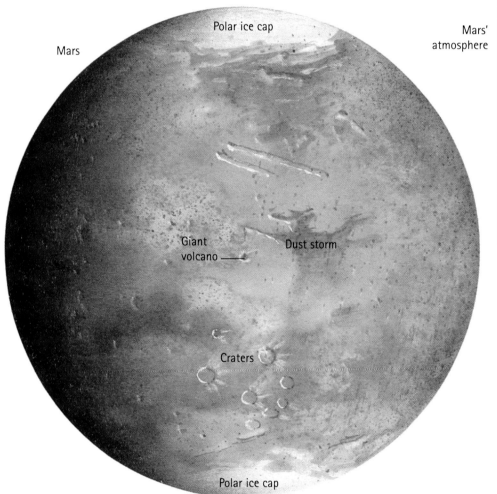

Mars

Polar ice cap

Giant volcano

Dust storm

Craters

Polar ice cap

Why is Mars called the 'Red Planet'?

Astronomers call Mars the 'Red Planet' because of its colour. Its surface is reddish-orange. This colour comes from the rust-like iron minerals in the surface rocks and soil.

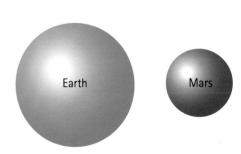

Earth

Mars

How is Mars made up?

Mars is a rocky planet and it has a similar make-up to Earth. It has a hard crust, a rocky mantle and an iron core. Its atmosphere, however, is very much thinner than Earth's. The atmospheric pressure on Mars is only about a hundredth of what it is on Earth. The main gas in the Martian atmosphere is carbon dioxide, instead of nitrogen and oxygen, as on Earth. There is very little moisture in the atmosphere, and no oceans, lakes or rivers. Around the cold poles, the moisture freezes to form the planet's ice caps. Although Mars is similar to Earth in some ways, it is a lot smaller.

MARS DATA

Diameter at equator: 6,787km
Average distance from Sun:
228 million km
Minimum distance from Earth:
56 million km
Turns on axis:
24 hours 37 minutes
Circles Sun: 687 Earth-days
Surface temperature:
-110°C to 0°C
Satellites: 2

Viking lander

The *Sojourner* rover

Deimos

Phobos

Does Mars have moons?

Mars has two small moons, Phobos and Deimos. Phobos is the larger, but it is less than 30 kilometres across. Astronomers believe they were once asteroids, captured by Mars' gravity.

Which space probes explored Mars?

In 1965, *Mariner 4* flew past Mars and sent back pictures. *Mariner 6* and *7* also flew past, and, in 1971, *Mariner 9* went into orbit round it. Five years later two *Viking* craft dropped landers onto the surface. In 1997, the *Pathfinder* probe landed, carrying a small vehicle called *Sojourner*, which investigated the surrounding rocks.

Dust storm

Olympus Mons and the surface of Mars

Mars' structure

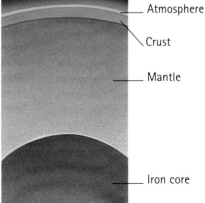

Atmosphere

Crust

Mantle

Iron core

What is Mars' surface like?

Mars' surface is dotted with vast deserts, craters and volcanoes. The highest volcano, Olympus Mons, is nearly 30 kilometres high. There is also a gash in the surface over 4,000 kilometres long and 7 kilometres deep in places. It has been called Mars' Grand Canyon, but its proper name is Mariner Valley. Smaller valleys look as if they have been made by flowing water, so astronomers think that Mars may once have had rivers and seas.

Quick-fire Quiz

1. What colour is Mars?
a) Yellow
b) Blue
c) Red

2. What is Mars' atmosphere made up of?
a) Oxygen
b) Carbon dioxide
c) Sulphur dioxide

3. What was the name of the Mars rover?
a) *Sojourner*
b) *Surveyor*
c) *Mariner*

4. What were Mars' moons originally?
a) Planets
b) Comets
c) Asteroids

31

Jupiter

Jupiter is the giant among the planets. All the others could fit into it with room to spare, and it could swallow more than 1,300 bodies the size of Earth. Jupiter is a gassy planet, made up mainly of hydrogen. Its stormy atmosphere is full of clouds. Jupiter travels through space with a large family of moons, some as big as planets.

What makes Jupiter so colourful?

The coloured 'stripes' we see on Jupiter are different kinds of clouds in the thick atmosphere. Because Jupiter spins round quickly, these clouds are drawn out into bands parallel with the equator. The paler bands are called zones and the darker ones are called belts.

The Great Red Spot

What is Jupiter made of?

Jupiter is a great ball of gas and liquid gas. Its atmosphere is more than 1,000 kilometres deep and is made up mainly of hydrogen gas, with some helium. It is full of clouds of ice, ammonia and ammonium compounds. At the bottom of the atmosphere the great pressure turns the hydrogen into a liquid. Deeper down, rapidly increasing pressure turns the hydrogen into a kind of liquid metal. Right at the centre, there is a small core of rock.

Jupiter's ring

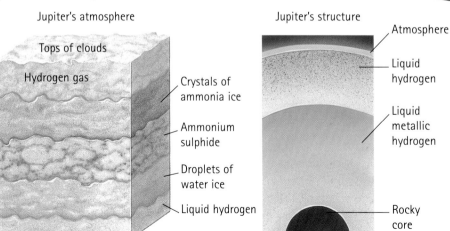

Jupiter's atmosphere

Tops of clouds

Hydrogen gas

Crystals of ammonia ice

Ammonium sulphide

Droplets of water ice

Liquid hydrogen

Jupiter's structure

Atmosphere

Liquid hydrogen

Liquid metallic hydrogen

Rocky core

The Great Red Spot

Europa

Callisto

Io

Ganymede

How many moons does Jupiter have?

Jupiter has at least 16 moons. We can see the four biggest with binoculars. The Italian astronomer Galileo discovered them in 1610, so they are known as the Galilean moons. In order of distance from Jupiter, they are Io, Europa, Ganymede and Callisto. With a diameter of 5,262 kilometres, Ganymede is the largest of Jupiter's moons and, at roughly the same size as planet Mercury, is the biggest moon in the Solar System. The smallest of Jupiter's moons, Leda, is about 15 kilometres across.

What is the Great Red Spot?

The most prominent feature on Jupiter's surface is a large red oval region called the Great Red Spot. Astronomers did not know what it was until space probes looked at it closely. We now know it is a gigantic swirling storm, rather like a huge hurricane on Earth. It measures about 40,000 kilometres across – three times the size of Earth.

Surface of Io

Erupting volcano

What's special about Io?

Io has been nicknamed the 'pizza moon' because it is so colourful. It is a very unusual moon because it has active volcanoes on it. These pour out liquid sulphur, which is a rich yellow-orange, giving Io its brilliant and varied colours. The *Voyager 1* probe discovered Io's volcanoes when it flew past Jupiter in 1979.

JUPITER DATA

Diameter at equator: 142,800km
Average distance from Sun: 778 million km
Minimum distance from Earth: 590 million km
Turns on axis: 9 hours 50 minutes
Circles Sun: 11.9 Earth-years
Temperature at cloud tops: -150°C
Satellites: 16 known

Which probes have visited Jupiter?

Pioneer 10 flew past Jupiter in 1973 and took the first close-up photographs of its colourful atmosphere. *Pioneer 11* followed the next year, and travelled on to Saturn. *Voyagers 1* and *2* flew past in 1979, sending back astounding pictures and information. In 1995, the *Galileo* probe went into orbit round Jupiter after dropping a probe into its atmosphere.

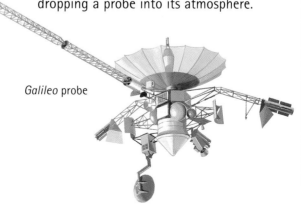

Galileo probe

Quick-fire Quiz

1. Which of these is Jupiter mainly made up of?
a) Rock
b) Carbon dioxide
c) Hydrogen

2. What is the Great Red Spot?
a) A storm
b) A sea
c) A sunspot

3. Which is Jupiter's biggest moon?
a) Io
b) Callisto
c) Ganymede

4. What makes Io colourful?
a) Its clouds
b) Its volcanoes
c) Its oceans

Saturn

Saturn is the second biggest planet, after Jupiter. Like Jupiter, it is a giant ball of gas. Saturn is a favourite planet among astronomers because of its shining rings. The rings appear to change shape year by year as the planet makes its way round the Sun.

SATURN DATA

Diameter at equator: 120,000km
Diameter of visible rings: 270,000km
Average distance from Sun:
   1,427 million km
Minimum distance from Earth:
   1,200 million km
Turns on axis: 10 hours 40 minutes
Circles Sun: 29.5 Earth-years
Temperature at cloud tops:
   -170°C
Satellites: 18 known

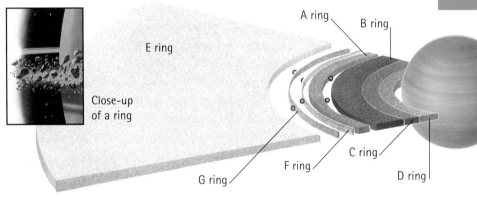

Close-up of a ring

E ring

A ring

B ring

G ring

F ring

C ring

D ring

What are Saturn's rings made of?

Saturn is surrounded by many rings, but only three can be seen from Earth – the A, B and C rings. The other rings were discovered by space probes. The rings look like solid sheets, but they are not. They are made up of millions upon millions of bits of ice, whizzing round the planet at high speed. The bits vary in size from specks of dust to large chunks. In places, the rings are less than 50 metres thick.

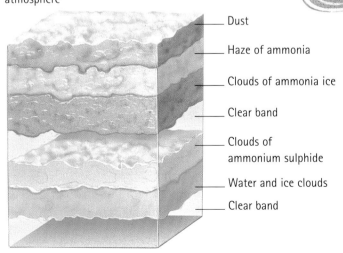

Saturn's atmosphere

Dust
Haze of ammonia
Clouds of ammonia ice
Clear band
Clouds of ammonium sulphide
Water and ice clouds
Clear band

Why is Saturn so cloudy?

Saturn is a very cloudy planet. The clouds form into bands parallel to the equator because the planet is spinning round so fast. These bands are not as easy to see as they are on Jupiter because of the haze that tops the atmosphere. There seem to be three main cloud layers on Saturn, located at different levels, with clear areas in between. The upper layers of clouds are made up of ammonia and ammonium compounds. At the lowest level, the clouds seem to be made up of water and ice particles, like the clouds we have on Earth.

What's Saturn like inside?

Saturn is a gas giant, which means that it is composed mainly of gas and liquid gas. Its cloudy atmosphere is made up almost entirely of hydrogen and helium. Below that lies a vast, deep ocean of liquid hydrogen. Deeper down is a layer of hydrogen in the form of a liquid metal. At the centre of the planet, there is a small core of rock.

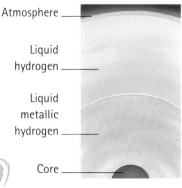

Atmosphere

Liquid hydrogen

Liquid metallic hydrogen

Core

Saturn's structure

Titan

What are Saturn's moons like?

Saturn has at least 18 moons – more than any other planet. Only five have a diameter greater than 1,000 kilometres – Tethys, Dione, Rhea, Titan and Iapetus. The smallest, Pan, is only about 20 kilometres across. Biggest by far is Titan. With a diameter of 5,140 kilometres, it is the second largest moon in the whole Solar System, and the only one that has a thick atmosphere.

Saturn

What is Titan's surface like?

Titan's thick atmosphere is made up mainly of nitrogen gas. It is orange in colour and full of hazy clouds that stop us seeing what its surface is like. Astronomers reckon that it may be covered with great lakes or seas of liquid methane, and there may be land areas covered with methane ice and snow. In 2004, the *Cassini* space probe will drop a landing probe (*Huygens*) on to the surface, which should tell us what conditions are like there.

Cassini

Saturn

The surface of Titan

Huygens landing probe

Uranus

Uranus is the third biggest planet, and is four times bigger across than Earth. It is so far from the Earth that it is barely visible with the naked eye. Because of this it was not discovered until the 1700s, with the help of a telescope.

Why is Uranus sometimes called the topsy-turvy planet?

All planets spin as they orbit the Sun. We say they spin round their axis (an imaginary line that goes through their north and south poles). In most planets the axis is nearly upright as the planet spins. But Uranus spins on an axis at right-angles to normal, so it is as if Uranus is lying on its side. This means that, at times in its orbit, Uranus' poles point straight at the Sun. As a result, they become hotter than the rest of the planet, instead of always being colder, as on Earth.

Who discovered Uranus?

In March 1781, an English astronomer named William Herschel was looking at the sky through a telescope. He spied what he thought must be a new comet, but it was actually a new planet. Until then, astronomers knew of only six planets. The new planet, which was later called Uranus, turned out to be twice as far away from the Sun as Saturn.

How many rings does Uranus have?

Astronomers used to think that Saturn was the only planet that had rings circling it. But, in 1977, they discovered that Uranus had rings too. There are about 11 main rings, made up of bits of rock up to a metre across, which whizz round the planet at high speed. The particles in some of the rings are kept in place by tiny 'shepherd' moons.

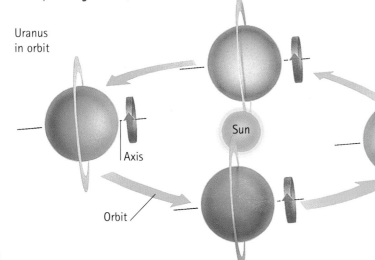

Uranus in orbit

Sun

Axis

Orbit

Direction of Uranus' rotation

Which probe has visited Uranus?

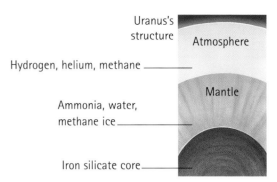

We can find out very little about Uranus through telescopes because it is so far away. Most of what we know comes from the *Voyager 2* space probe, which visited Uranus in 1986. *Voyager 2* had earlier visited Jupiter (1979) and Saturn (1981). It has now gone far beyond the planets, and will soon leave the Solar System and begin a journey to the stars.

Voyager 2

Uranus's structure

Atmosphere

Hydrogen, helium, methane

Mantle

Ammonia, water, methane ice

Iron silicate core

What is Uranus made of?

Uranus has a thick atmosphere of hydrogen, helium and methane, and a mantle of water, ammonia and methane ice. At the centre there is an iron silicate core.

What are Uranus' moons like?

We can only see the five largest of Uranus' moons from Earth – Miranda, Ariel, Umbriel, Titania and Oberon. Ten smaller moons were discovered by *Voyager 2*. The large moons are great balls of rock and ice, pitted with craters, and with long cracks in their surface. Titania is the biggest moon. It is about 1,600 kilometres across.

Miranda

Ariel

Titania

URANUS DATA

Diameter at equator:
51,000km
Average distance from Sun:
2,870 million km
Minimum distance from Earth: 2,600 million km
Turns on axis:
17 hours 14 minutes
Circles Sun: 84 Earth-years
Temperature at cloud tops:
-200°C
Satellites: 15

What is special about Miranda?

Miranda is the smallest moon that can be seen from Earth, with a diameter of only about 500 kilometres. Close-up photographs show it to be the most interesting moon of all. Its surface is a patchwork of different kinds of landscape - craters, grooves, cliffs and valleys. Astronomers think that, ages ago, Miranda shattered into pieces when it collided with another body. Then the pieces came together to create the landscape we see today.

The surface of Miranda

Quick-fire Quiz

1. What makes Uranus unique?
a) It has many moons
b) Its large size
c) A highly tilted axis

2. What do shepherd moons keep in place?
a) Space sheep
b) Meteorites
c) Ring particles

3. When was Uranus discovered?
a) In 1681
b) In 1781
c) In 1881

4. Which is Uranus' biggest moon?
a) Miranda
b) Ariel
c) Titania

Neptune and Pluto

Neptune and Pluto were the last planets to be discovered. They lie thousands of millions of kilometres away from Earth, at the edge of the Solar System. Neptune is a gas giant, very like Uranus. Pluto is a tiny ice ball, smaller than our own Moon.

Why is Neptune blue?

Neptune is a lovely blue colour, rather like Earth. This colour comes about because the atmosphere contains a gas called methane. Methane absorbs the red colours in sunlight, and makes the light coming from Neptune's atmosphere appear blue. Dark spots that sometimes appear in Neptune's atmosphere are violent storms.

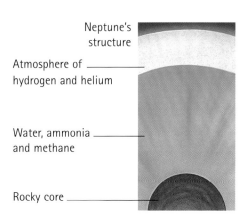

Neptune's structure

Atmosphere of hydrogen and helium

Water, ammonia and methane

Rocky core

Does Neptune have moons?

Through a telescope, we can see two moons circling around Neptune – Triton and Nereid. When *Voyager 2* visited the planet, it found six more. One, Proteus, was slightly bigger than Nereid, but the others were tiny. As the picture shows, Triton is by far the biggest moon, measuring some 2,700 kilometres across. Unusually, it circles the planet in the opposite direction from most moons.

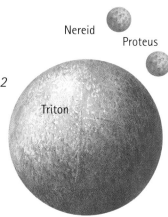

Nereid

Proteus

Triton

What is Neptune like?

Neptune has a similar make-up to its twin planet, Uranus. It has an atmosphere made up mainly of hydrogen, together with some helium. Beneath this there is a huge, deep, hot ocean of water and liquid gases, including methane. In the centre, there is a core of rock, which may be about the same size as Earth.

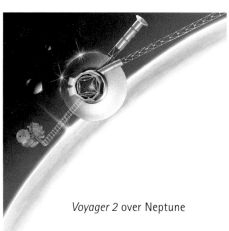

Voyager 2 over Neptune

When did Voyager 2 visit Neptune?

Neptune was the last planet *Voyager 2* visited on its 12-year journey. Launched in 1977, *Voyager 2* passed about 5,000 kilometres above Neptune's cloud tops on August 24, 1989 – closer than to any other planet. By then, it was more than 4,000 million kilometres from Earth, and its radio signals took more than four hours to get back.

NEPTUNE DATA

Diameter at equator:
49,500km

Average distance from Sun:
4,500 million km

Minimum distance from Earth:
4,300 million km

Turns on axis: 17 hours 6 minutes

Circles Sun: 165 Earth-years

Temperature at cloud tops:
-210°C

Satellites: 8

PLUTO DATA

Diameter at equator: 2,250km

Average distance from Sun:
5,900 million km

Minimum distance from Earth:
4,300 million km

Turns on axis: 6 Earth-days 9 hours

Circles Sun: 248 Earth-years

Surface temperature: -230°C

Satellites: 1

Charon

What is special about Charon?

Pluto's only moon, Charon, is unique in the Solar System, as it is half as big across as Pluto itself. No other moon is as big compared with its planet. Also, it circles Pluto in the same time it takes Pluto to spin round once. This makes Charon appear fixed in Pluto's sky.

Pluto

What do we know about Pluto?

We do not know much about Pluto because it is so far away. At its furthest, it travels more than 7,000 million kilometres from the Sun. Even in powerful telescopes, it looks only like a faint star. So far, no space probes have visited the planet. All we know is that Pluto is a deep-frozen ball of rock and ice. It probably has a covering of 'snow', made up of frozen methane gas.

Pluto's structure

Thin atmosphere of methane and nitrogen ___

Mantle of ice ___

Rocky core ___

Who found Pluto?

United States astronomer Percival Lowell built his own observatory, and led a search for a ninth planet. An astronomer who worked there, Clyde Tombaugh, finally discovered it in 1930.

Percival Lowell

What would Charon look like from Pluto?

Because it appears fixed in Pluto's sky, Charon can only be seen from one side of the planet. From that side, Charon would appear huge, much bigger than the Moon does on Earth. This is because Charon circles very close to Pluto, only about 20,000 kilometres away. Our Moon circles 20 times further from us.

Quick-fire Quiz

1. Which is largest?
a) Charon
b) Neptune
c) Pluto

2. Which is Neptune's biggest moon?
a) Charon
b) Nereid
c) Triton

3. Who discovered Pluto?
a) Percival Lowell
b) Clyde Tombaugh
c) William Herschel

4. *Voyager 2* reached Neptune from Earth after how long?
a) 5 years
b) 9 years
c) 12 years

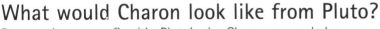

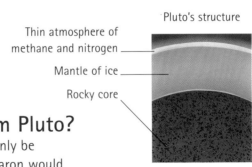

Asteroids and Meteoroids

There are many bodies in the Solar System besides the planets and their moons. They are mostly lumps of rock or ice. The biggest ones, called asteroids, can be hundreds of kilometres across. The smallest, called meteoroids, can be as tiny as grains of sand.

How big are asteroids?

Ceres, the biggest asteroid, is about 1,000 kilometres across. It was discovered in 1801. Pallas and Vesta are about 550 kilometres across. Most asteroids are just a few tens of kilometres across.

Ceres

A meteor

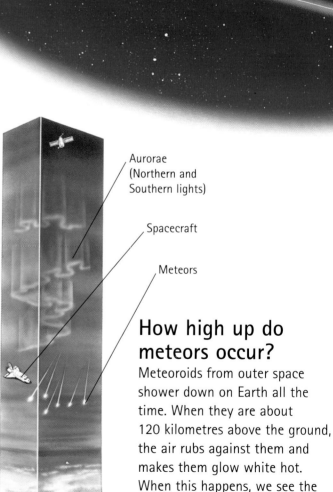

What is a fireball?

Most of the meteoroids that enter Earth's atmosphere are tiny specks. But some are as big as pebbles. These larger meteoroids burn for longer and more brightly, and create the flaming objects we call fireballs.

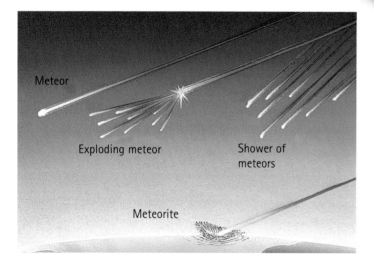

Meteor

Exploding meteor

Shower of meteors

Meteorite

What is the difference between a meteor and a meteorite?

Meteoroids are invisible unless they collide with the Earth's atmosphere, when they become streaks of light, known as meteors or 'shooting stars'. When a group of meteoroids all burn together, we see a meteor shower. Meteorites are simply meteors that have fallen to Earth. Some are made of rock, others mainly of the metals iron and nickel.

Aurorae (Northern and Southern lights)

Spacecraft

Meteors

How high up do meteors occur?

Meteoroids from outer space shower down on Earth all the time. When they are about 120 kilometres above the ground, the air rubs against them and makes them glow white hot. When this happens, we see the streaks of light we call meteors.

Where do you find asteroids?

Most asteroids are found in a broad ring about midway between the orbits of Mars and Jupiter. Astronomers call the ring the asteroid belt. But some asteroids travel outside the belt. A few occasionally come dangerously close to Earth. Two small groups of asteroids, the Trojans, circle the Sun in Jupiter's orbit. The picture below shows the orbits of some of the more unusual asteroids.

Where did the asteroids come from?

Until quite recently, astronomers believed that the asteroids were the remains of another planet. They believed that this planet came too close to Jupiter and was pulled apart by Jupiter's gravity. But astronomers today think that the asteroids are a collection of lumps that never gathered together to form a planet or a moon.

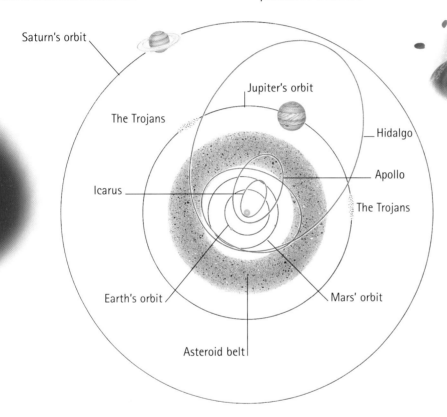

Saturn's orbit

Jupiter's orbit

The Trojans

Hidalgo

Apollo

Icarus

The Trojans

Earth's orbit

Mars' orbit

Asteroid belt

Did a meteor kill the dinosaurs?

When meteorites or asteroids fall to Earth, they create pits, or craters. Big meteorites can create enormous craters, like the famous Meteor Crater in Arizona, United States. This measures more than 1,200 metres across and is about 180 metres deep. A huge crater near the Mexican coast was formed 65 million years ago by a falling asteroid. Many scientists think the impact changed Earth's climate, killing the dinosaurs and many other species.

Arizona Meteor Crater

Quick-fire Quiz

1. What is a shooting star?
a) An exploding star
b) An asteroid
c) A meteor

2. Which of these hit the ground?
a) Fireballs
b) Meteorites
c) Meteors

3. Which is the biggest asteroid?
a) Vesta
b) Arizona
c) Ceres

4. What do asteroids circle round?
a) The Sun
b) Jupiter
c) Saturn

Comets

Comets are small members of the Solar System. They are lumps of ice and dust. Most of the time, they are found in the outermost parts of the Solar System, where we cannot see them. They only become visible when they travel in towards the Sun and start to melt. Then they may become bright enough to shine like beacons in the sky.

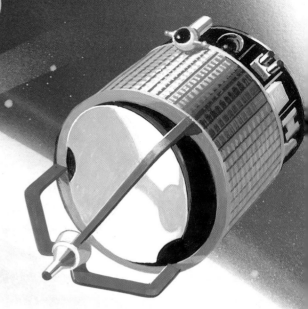

Which probes have visited comets?

Giotto was one of five space probes sent to meet Halley's comet in 1986. Launched by the European Space Agency, it sent back close-up pictures of the comet's head and nucleus. Two other probes (*Vega 1* and *Vega 2*) were sent by Russia and two (*Sakigake* and *Suisei*) were sent by Japan.

Edmond Halley

Which is the most famous comet?

Halley's comet is probably the most famous of all the comets. It was named after the English astronomer Edmond Halley (1656–1742). He saw a comet in 1682, and reckoned that it was the same one that had been seen in 1531 and 1607. He suggested that it turned up about every 76 years, and would do so again in 1758. It did exactly as he had predicted and, since then, it has been called Halley's comet. Ancient records show that Halley's comet has been seen regularly since 240 BC. It appeared last in 1986, and it will return next in 2061. In 1986, it was only just visible to the naked eye. Two more recent comets, Hyakutake in 1996 and Hale-Bopp in 1997, were very much brighter.

Why do comets have tails?

When a comet is a long way from the Sun we cannot see it, and it is frozen solid. As it travels in towards the Sun, it warms up. Some of its icy surface melts and turns to gas. This mixes with escaping dust to form a cloud. The cloud shines in the sunlight, and the comet becomes visible. As the comet gets nearer the Sun, the gas and dust cloud gets bigger. The sunlight exerts a kind of pressure that forces the gas and dust away from the comet's head, forming a tail. After the comet has looped round the Sun, it begins to cool. Its shining head and tail shrink and fade away.

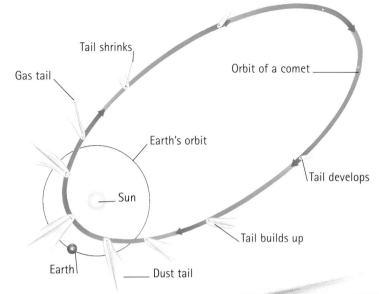

Tail shrinks

Gas tail

Orbit of a comet

Earth's orbit

Sun

Tail develops

Tail builds up

Earth

Dust tail

How big is the comet's nucleus?

As it travels across the sky, a comet may stretch for hundreds of thousands of kilometres. That is the size of the billowing cloud of gas and dust that forms the comet's head and tail. The solid part of the comet, its nucleus, is very much smaller and only a few kilometres across.

Crumbling particles of rock and ice

Jets of gas given off

Nucleus

Quick-fire Quiz

1. What makes comets have tails?
a) Gravity
b) Sunlight
c) Starlight

2. When was Halley's comet first recorded?
a) 2000 BC
b) 240 BC
c) AD 1066

3. A comet has recently hit which planet?
a) Jupiter
b) Neptune
c) Mars

4. Which is the smallest part of a comet?
a) Head
b) Tail
c) Nucleus

Can comets hit the planets?

On its way in towards the Sun, a comet may travel close to one of the planets. When this happens, the comet is pulled from its normal path by the planet's gravity. If the comet gets too close, it will end up hitting the planet. In 1994, pieces of a broken-up comet named Shoemaker Levy 9 smashed into the planet Jupiter. Each time a piece hit the atmosphere, it created a great fireball, which blasted out great clouds of gas.

43

DINOSAURS

Digging up the Facts

Millions of years ago dinosaurs ruled the Earth, but they died out long before people existed. We only know about dinosaurs from their fossils – animal and plant remains that have been preserved in rocks, and which we can still see today.

How are fossils dug up?

When a dinosaur fossil is found, fossil experts, called palaeontologists, carefully clear away the overlying rocks. They photograph, measure and record the position of each bone. Then the bones are dug up, wrapped in layers of paper and plaster and left to dry. This plaster 'coat' protects the fossil on its journey to the museum, where the fossil is rebuilt. Sometimes a whole dinosaur skeleton is put together in this way.

How is a fossil formed?

When an animal or plant dies, it usually rots away. However, if it is buried quickly by mud or sand, parts of it may survive. Over millions of years it will turn into a fossil.

1 A dinosaur dies and its flesh is eaten or rots away.

2 Its skeleton is covered by layers of mud or sand.

3 Slowly, mud turns to rock, and bones become fossils.

4 As the rock wears away, the fossil is revealed.

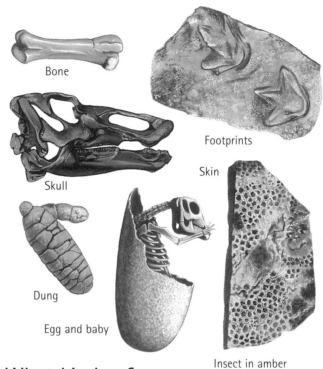

Bone

Footprints

Skull

Skin

Dung

Egg and baby

Insect in amber

What kinds of fossils are there?

Fossil bones and teeth are not the only dinosaur remains. Fossil imprints of their scaly skin, footprints and nests of eggs have all been found. Scientists can even tell what dinosaurs ate from their fossilized dung. Some fossils form in other ways. For example, an insect trapped in the sticky resin of a tree can be fossilized when the resin turns into hard amber.

George Cuvier   Mary Mantell   Gideon Mantell   Richard Owen   Edwin Cope   Othniel Marsh

One name or two?

Dinosaur names are in Latin and have two parts – the genus name and the species name. They are written in italics and the genus name has a capital letter, e.g. *Tyrannosaurus rex*. Similar species of dinosaur are put in the same genus, which is the name usually used.

Who found the first dinosaur bones?

Dinosaur bones were first found hundreds of years ago, but people thought they were from giants or dragons. In 1822, Georges Cuvier suggested they belonged to giant reptiles. In 1824, William Buckland named the first dinosaur *Megalosaurus* (big lizard). A year later, fossil hunters Mary and Gideon Mantell named a second dinosaur, *Iguanodon*. Then, in 1842, Richard Owen called them 'dinosaurs', meaning 'terrible lizards'. In America over 130 new kinds of dinosaur were found by Edward Cope and Othniel Marsh.

William Buckland

47

Colour and Camouflage

No-one knows for sure what colour dinosaurs were. A few pieces of fossil dinosaur skin have been found, but the colour faded millions of years ago. Perhaps they had similar colours to reptiles today.

What use are colours?

Skin colour can help animals to hide, to attract a mate or to act as a warning. Many dinosaurs were probably camouflaged. Their skins may have been patterned to blend in with their surroundings. *Deinonychus* could have been sand-coloured, like lions today, to blend in with the sandy ground or dry, yellow plants. Or perhaps *Deinonychus* were striped like tigers so that they could hide among the vegetation until the pack was ready to attack.

Deinonychus

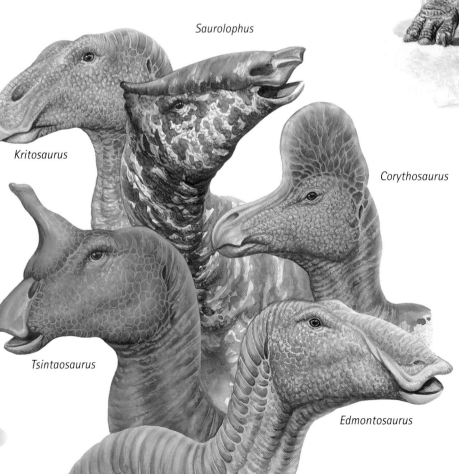

Saurolophus

Kritosaurus

Corythosaurus

Tsintaosaurus

Edmontosaurus

Could dinosaurs see in colour?

No-one knows for sure. We do know that some dinosaurs, called hadrosaurs, had crests, frills and inflatable air sacs on their heads. The hadrosaurs' heads and crests were probably brightly coloured so that they could be seen easily. Perhaps the dinosaurs also used their crests to send signals to each other. Several modern-day reptiles send signals in this way, so it is likely that some dinosaurs could see colours.

Were male and female dinosaurs different colours?

Mallard ducks

It is quite possible that they were. The male and female adults of many animals today, including some birds and lizards, are very differently coloured. The male may use his bright colours to attract a female or to warn off other males. Females may have dull, drab colours so they are less easy to spot when sitting on eggs or looking after babies. When artists first started drawing dinosaurs they tended to make them all brown or green, but now dinosaurs are often shown with very colourful markings.

Parasaurolophus

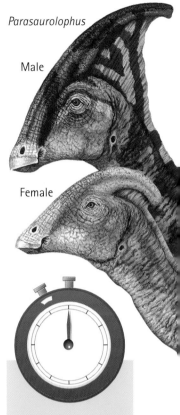

Male

Female

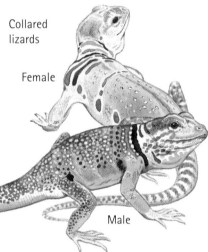

Collared lizards

Female

Male

Smooth or scaly?

Fossils and mummified skin show that many dinosaurs had skin covered with lumps and bumps for protection. Several colourful reptiles today have similar skins, so some experts think dinosaurs were also brightly coloured.

Striped dinosaurs?

A zebra's stripes breaks up its outline, making it hard for a predator to pick one animal out from the herd. Dinosaurs which lived in herds may have had stripes for the same reason.

Quick-fire Quiz

1. Which of these had a large crest?
   a) *Deinonychus*
   b) *Corythosaurus*
   c) *Kritosaurus*

2. Why was dinosaur skin bumpy?
   a) For protection
   b) For warmth
   c) For camouflage

3. Why might dinosaurs have had stripes?
   a) To show off
   b) To confuse predators
   c) To attract mates

4. What is camouflage?
   a) Blending in with the surroundings
   b) Changing colour
   c) Having bright warning colours

Dinosaur Giants

Dinosaurs are the biggest land animals that have ever lived on Earth. The largest were the plant-eating sauropods. There were several kinds and they all had enormous bodies, long necks and small heads. Some were as tall as a four-storey building.

Which is the largest complete fossil dinosaur?

The biggest almost complete skeleton found so far is that of *Brachiosaurus*. This dinosaur was so tall it could raise its head 13 metres above the ground. One *Brachiosaurus* would have weighed as much as ten large elephants.

Which was the heaviest dinosaur?

Only a few bones of *Supersaurus* and *Ultrasaurus* have been found but they both outweigh *Brachiosaurus*. *Ultrasaurus* holds the record at almost 30 metres long, 12 metres high and up to 130 tonnes in weight. That is as heavy as 20 large elephants.

Brachiosaurus

Diplodocus

Apatosaurus

The huge sauropods were many times bigger than today's largest land animal, the elephant.

Which dinosaurs had the heaviest bones?

Sauropod dinosaurs had the biggest and heaviest bones. A thigh bone weighing 450 kilograms has been found. Early fossil-hunters struggled to get their finds home. Now helicopters are often used.

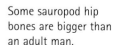
Some sauropod hip bones are bigger than an adult man.

Were dinosaurs brainy?

Dinosaurs may have been big, but they were not all very bright. Most of them, like this *Stegosaurus*, had a small brain. Weight for weight, *Brachiosaurus* had the smallest brain of almost any known dinosaur. Its brain weighed only one hundred thousandth of its body weight. You are much brainier: a human brain weighs a fortieth of an adult's body weight. But fossils show us that some dinosaurs had much bigger brains and were probably quite smart.

How big did dinosaurs grow?

It is hard to work out the size of the biggest dinosaurs because only a few bones have been found. Experts think that *Ultrasaurus* was the heaviest and that *Seismosaurus* was the longest (39–52 metres). That's longer than a blue whale – the biggest animal alive today.

Blue whale

Which was the biggest carnivore?

Tyrannosaurus rex was one of the biggest meat-eating dinosaurs. It grew up to 14 metres long and over 5 metres high. Its head alone was over a metre in length. It could have opened its mouth wide enough to swallow you whole!

Quick Fire Quiz

1. How long was *Tyrannosaurus'* head?
a) Over 10m
b) Over 2m
c) Over 1m

2. Which dinosaurs lived under water?
a) None of them
b) *Stegosaurus*
c) *Brachiosaurus*

3. Which is the most complete sauropod skeleton?
a) *Brachiosaurus*
b) *Tyrannosaurus*
c) *Ultrasaurus*

4. What is the biggest animal alive today?
a) Elephant
b) *Seismosaurus*
c) Blue whale

Which dinosaur had the biggest feet?

The front feet of sauropods such as *Brachiosaurus* were huge — up to a metre long. Some fossilized sauropod footprints are big enough to sit in. A sauropod's feet had to be big to support the dinosaur's great weight. Palaeontologists can work out an animal's size, weight and speed from its footprints.

No dinosaur could ever really have lived like this.

Did dinosaurs live under water?

No. People once thought that *Brachiosaurus* was too big to live on land. They thought it supported its weight by living in water and breathing through the nostrils on the top of its head. We now know this was not true. The pressure of the water would have crushed its ribs and stopped *Brachiosaurus* from breathing.

51

Small Dinosaurs

Not all dinosaurs were huge. Some were as small as modern-day lizards. Fewer fossils of small dinosaurs have been found because they were often eaten by other dinosaurs and their fragile bones were easily broken.

What did small dinosaurs eat?

1 Some small dinosaurs ate plants, while others fed on insects, worms or small reptiles. Tiny *Lesothosaurus* lived in herds and fed on plants. It relied on speed to outrun predators.

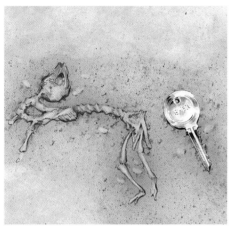

What is the smallest dinosaur skeleton?

A *Mussaurus* (mouse-lizard) skeleton found in Argentina in South America was tiny enough to fit into the palm of your hand. The skeleton was a baby dinosaur with a big head, eyes and feet. Small eggs, about 2.5 centimetres long, were found nearby. An adult *Mussaurus* would have been about 3 metres long.

Which were the smallest dinosaurs?

One of the earliest and smallest meat-eating dinosaurs was *Saltopus*. At just 60 centimetres long its body was the same size as that of a large chicken. *Saltopus* was a speedy hunter and could catch fast-moving lizards and flying insects. In 1984, a small plant-eating dinosaur, *Leaellynasaura*, was found in Australia. It was about the same size as *Saltopus*. However, some scientists think that the fossils were not fully grown and that adult *Leaellynasaura* may have been up to 2 metres long.

Leaellynasaura

Saltopus

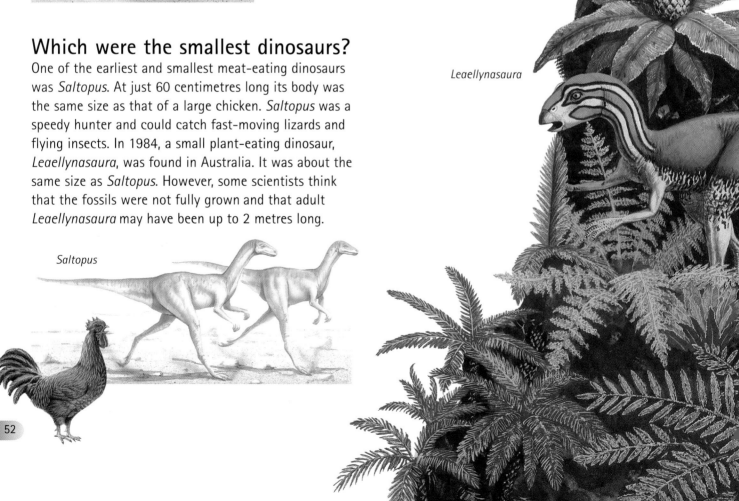

2 *Compsognathus* was the size of a large pet cat. It moved quickly, using its speed to catch fast-moving prey like insects and lizards. One fossil *Compsognathus* skeleton has been found with the remains of its last meal, a lizard, inside it.

3 *Hypsilophodon* was a speedy little dinosaur that grew to about 2 metres long. It lived in forests and used its horny beak to nip off juicy shoots from plants.

4 Wolf-sized *Oviraptor* may have darted along at up to 50 kilometres an hour. It hunted lizards and small mammals and raided other dinosaurs' nests to snatch the eggs.

How big were dinosaur babies?

Newly hatched dinosaur babies were very small. You could have held this baby *Protoceratops* in your hand. One baby *Troodon* fossil has been found that is only 7 centimetres long — the size of a large hen's egg.

Did small dinosaurs defend themselves?

Scutellosaurus was only the size of a cat, but this little plant-eater was no easy meal for big dinosaurs. It was protected by rows of small bony knobs along its back and tail, and was the smallest armour-plated dinosaur.

Dinosaur Babies

Less than 100 years ago, scientists were not sure how dinosaur babies were born. In 1923, an expedition to the Gobi Desert in Mongolia found a nest of fossilized dinosaur eggs, laid over 100 million years earlier. This proved that dinosaurs laid eggs on land.

Who found the first eggs?

Roy Chapman Andrews discovered the first dinosaur eggs in 1923 in the Gobi Desert. He worked for the American Museum of Natural History and led many exciting dinosaur-hunting expeditions. He even used specially adapted cars to drive across the Gobi desert. Some people think he was the original 'Indiana Jones'.

How big were dinosaurs' eggs?

Dinosaur eggs were laid in clutches of ten to 40. Their size varied according to the size of the adult, but the eggs were small for such large animals. For example, a 30-metre long female probably laid eggs about 60 centimetres long. A really huge egg was not possible because it would need such a thick shell the baby could not break out of it.

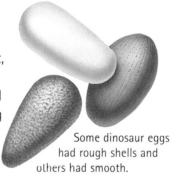

Some dinosaur eggs had rough shells and others had smooth.

Did dinosaurs build nests?

1 Some dinosaurs, such as the *Maiasaura*, certainly built nests. *Maiasaura* lived in herds. Every year the females gathered at the same nesting site. We know this because a huge nesting area has been found in Montana, United States.

Did dinosaurs look after their babies?

Experts think that some kinds of baby dinosaurs, such as young *Maiasaura*, were not very well developed. The adults probably fed their newly hatched young on soft plant shoots until they were able to fend for themselves. The babies of other dinosaurs, such as *Orodromeus*, were well developed and could probably run soon after they hatched. So perhaps, like many reptiles today, these dinosaurs laid lots of eggs and left their hatchlings to look after themselves.

2 Female *Maiasaura* made a low mound of mud about 2 metres across. Each female dug out a nest and lined it with twigs and leaves.

Did dinosaurs egg sit?

In 1993, 70 years after Roy Chapman Andrews found the first dinosaur eggs, another expedition set out for the Gobi Desert. This time, the scientists discovered the fossilized remains of an *Oviraptor* sitting on a nest of eggs. The find proved that some kinds of dinosaurs sat on their eggs to hatch them, in the same way that birds do today.

Quick-fire Quiz

1. Where were the first eggs found?
a) Sahara Desert
b) Gobi Desert
c) Kalahari Desert

2. Which dinosaur stole eggs?
a) *Troodon*
b) *Triceratops*
c) *Maiasaura*

3. Who found the first eggs?
a) Indiana Jones
b) Richard Owen
c) Roy Chapman Andrews

4. What were *Maiasaura* nests made of?
a) Stones
b) Mud
c) Paper

Did dinosaurs defend their young?

Armoured dinosaurs like *Triceratops* may have defended their young by charging a would-be predator. Scientists think a herd of adult plant-eaters on the move defended their young by keeping them in the middle of the herd.

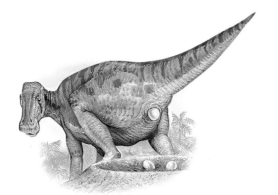

3 Each female laid about 20 to 25 eggs in the nest. She covered them with more plants to keep them warm.

4 The *Maiasaura* mother guarded her eggs carefully. Egg-thieves, such as *Troodon*, were always ready to snatch an easy meal.

5 The *Maiasaura* hatchlings broke out of their egg shells using a special sharp tooth on their snouts.

Communication

Animals cannot talk to each other, so they communicate in other ways. They use sounds, smells, touch and visual signals to tell each other what is going on. Dinosaurs may have used similar methods to send 'messages' to one another.

What sounds did dinosaurs make?

Dinosaurs had complex ears and could probably hear well, so they may have used many different sounds to send signals to each other. Like reptiles alive today, most dinosaurs could probably hiss or grunt and large ones may have roared. A few, like the hadrosaurs, probably made distinctive calls to each other through their horns, crests and inflatable nose flaps. Scientists believe this is possible because, when they blew through models of different hadrosaur skulls, they found that each skull gave a different sound.

Tsintaosaurus

Edmontosaurus

Lambeosaurus

Corythosaurus

Male peacock displaying

Why was making a noise useful?

Dinosaurs may have used sound to warn of danger or keep in touch with other members of a large herd. *Parasaurolophus* may have hooted a warning if danger threatened. The duck-billed dinosaur *Edmontosaurus* may have blown up a bag of skin over its nose and bellowed loudly at rival males. Young dinosaurs may have squeaked to get an adult's attention.

Did dinosaurs display like birds?

Experts think that some male dinosaurs displayed to the females during the mating season. Just as peacocks display their coloured feathers, male dinosaurs may have displayed bright head crests, spines or neck ruffs to attract females and warn off rival males.

Did dinosaurs use their noses?

Fossils of dinosaurs' brains suggest that many dinosaurs had a good sense of smell and most dinosaurs had well-developed nostrils. A strong sense of smell would have helped dinosaurs sniff out food. If, as some scientists think, dinosaurs gave off scent signals, they may also have used their sense of smell to find a mate. *Brachiosaurus* had huge nostrils on the top of its head. No-one knows why, but perhaps they allowed it to eat water plants and breathe at the same time.

Brachiosaurus

Parasaurolophus herd

Quick-fire Quiz

1. Which dinosaur group had head crests?
   a) Hadrosaurs
   b) Theropods
   c) Lizards

2. Which dinosaur had an inflatable nose flap?
   a) *Edmontosaurus*
   b) *Brachiosaurus*
   c) *Lambeosaurus*

3. Which dinosaur had a hollow crest?
   a) *Tyrannosaurus*
   b) *Brachiosaurus*
   c) *Parasaurolophus*

4. Where were *Brachiosaurus'* nostrils?
   a) On the end of its nose
   b) It didn't have any
   c) On top of its head

How did noisy noses work?

Hadrosaurs such as *Parasaurolophus* and *Lambeosaurus* had hollow crests. Air passages extended from the nose through the crest and down into the throat. The dinosaurs could hoot and honk as they breathed in and out. Different types of crest produced different notes.

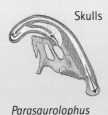
Skulls
Parasaurolophus

Lambeosaurus

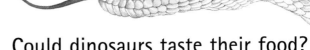

Could dinosaurs taste their food?

Many dinosaurs had tongues and they could probably taste and smell their food, like most animals today. Reptiles such as snakes use their forked tongue to 'taste' the air for traces of prey. But there is no evidence to suggest that any dinosaurs had tongues that could do this.

Plant-Eaters

Most dinosaurs were herbivores. They ate plants not meat. Plant-eating dinosaurs came in all shapes and sizes from small two-legged dinosaurs to huge sauropods. Plants are hard to digest so, to get enough energy from their food, many spent most of the day eating.

Lizard or bird hips?

Experts divide dinosaurs into two groups by the shape of their hips. Sauropod plant-eaters (1) had lizard hips. Their big stomachs unbalanced them so they had to walk on four legs. Two-legged theropod meat-eaters (2) also had lizard hips. Plant-eating bird-hipped dinosaurs (3) evolved later. Many walked on two legs with their big stomach slung between their back legs. Armoured bird-hipped plant-eaters were so heavy that they walked on four legs.

1

2

3

Psittacosaurus

Did dinosaurs eat leaves?

Leaves were the main diet of many plant-eaters. *Psittacosaurus* probably snipped leaves off with its bird-like beak, then sliced them into smaller bits with its scissor-like teeth. Like the giraffe, *Brachiosaurus* used its long neck to graze on leafy treetops.

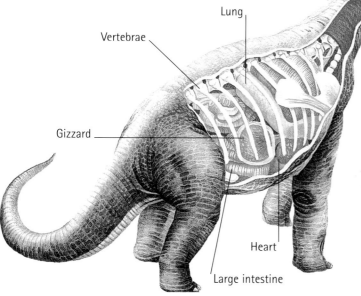

Lung

Vertebrae

Gizzard

Heart

Large intestine

Why were sauropods so big?

A sauropod's huge body was filled almost entirely with its guts. Sauropods like *Brachiosaurus* ate up to 200 kilograms of plants a day, so they needed a big stomach and long intestines to digest this tough food. Until recently, experts had to guess what a dinosaur's insides looked like, but in 1998 two dinosaurs from China were found with their guts intact. These should tell us more about what dinosaurs ate.

Lufengosaurus

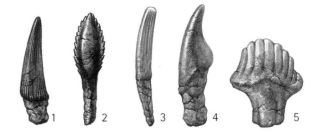

1   2   3   4   5

Did plant-eaters have teeth?

Most plant-eating dinosaurs had teeth, and experts can tell what food a dinosaur ate by looking at these. *Lufengosaurus*, an early sauropod, had many small peg-like teeth with jagged edges. These were great for nipping off soft leaves, but no use for chewing, so it swallowed its food whole.

Why were teeth different shapes?

The size and shape of a dinosaur's teeth depended on what it ate. The ornithopod *Heterodontosaurus* had sharp, narrow front teeth (1) for cutting and slicing. *Plateosaurus* (2) and sauropods like *Diplodocus* (3) and *Apatosaurus* (4) had peg-like teeth to shred and crush food. *Stegosaurus* (5) had leaf-shaped teeth for slicing and munching soft plants.

Why did dinosaurs swallow stones?

Small stones have been found in the rib cages of many dinosaurs. Few dinosaurs could move their jaws from side to side, so they could not chew their food. They swallowed it whole and probably swallowed small stones (gastroliths) to help them grind food as it churned about in their stomachs. Chickens swallow grit to do the same thing.

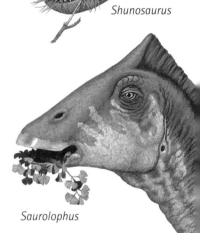

Shunosaurus

Did dinosaurs eat grass?

Grasses did not develop on Earth until 25 million years after the dinosaurs died out. Instead, herbivorous dinosaurs ate other plants that were around at the time. Long-necked sauropods such as *Shunosaurus* used their simple peg-like teeth to munch on leaves, pine needles and juicy shoots. A hadrosaur such as *Saurolophus* ate leaves from flowering plants and crunchy pine cones. It chopped off the leaves with its horny beak, then chewed them with its flat back teeth. Horned dinosaurs like *Triceratops* sliced up tough ferns and horsetails with their sharp beaks and teeth.

Leaves, pine needles and shoots

Pine cones and shrub leaves

Ferns and horsetails

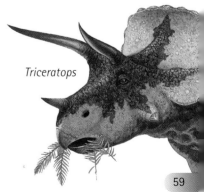

Saurolophus

Triceratops

Meat-Eaters

All meat-eating, or carnivorous, dinosaurs were theropods. (Theropod means 'beast foot'.) They walked on two legs and their three toes were armed with sharp claws. Some were fierce hunters, chasing and killing their prey. Others were scavengers, feeding on dead animals.

Did dinosaurs have sharp teeth?
The sharp, backward pointing teeth of *Megalosaurus* are typical of many large meat-eating dinosaurs. They were good for gripping and ripping their prey. Other carnivorous dinosaurs had small sharp teeth or crushing beaks.

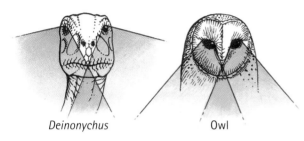

Deinonychus   *Owl*

Did meat-eaters have sharp eyesight?
Many hunters such as *Deinonychus* had good eyesight. It may have had forward-facing eyes and good binocular (overlapping) vision like modern owls. This would have given it a single view of its prey and helped it judge distances.

Did all meat-eaters look the same?
Meat-eating dinosaurs came in all shapes and sizes. They ranged in size from chicken-sized *Saltopus* (60 centimetres) to huge *Tyrannosaurus* (12 metres long). Big theropods like *Tyrannosaurus*, *Allosaurus* and *Dilophosaurus* hunted large plant-eaters, while speedy *Troodon* killed small reptiles and mammals. *Struthiomimus*, *Avimimus* and *Oviraptor* used their strong beaks to catch and crush insects and eggs.

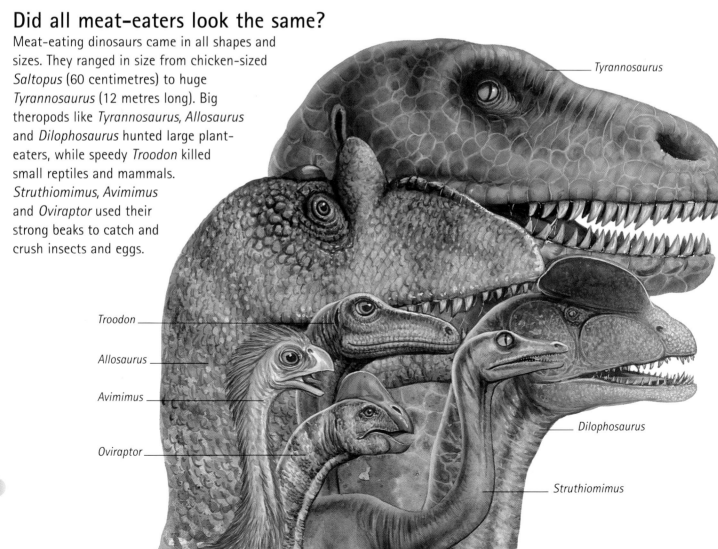

Tyrannosaurus

Troodon

Allosaurus

Avimimus

Oviraptor

Dilophosaurus

Struthiomimus

Did dinosaurs eat fish?

Experts believe that dinosaurs such as *Baryonyx* snapped up fish with their long crocodile-like jaws. *Baryonyx* may also have speared fish with the huge hook-like claw on its front feet, just as brown bears do today.

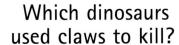

Which dinosaurs used claws to kill?

Deinonychus ('terrible claw') and its relatives used their claws to kill much larger animals. *Deinonychus* leapt at its victims, slashing them with the deadly 12 centimetres long claw on the second toe of its back foot.

Did dinosaurs hunt in packs?

Like today's wolves, some small meat-eating dinosaurs, such as *Deinonychus,* hunted in packs. This would have allowed them to hunt larger prey such as a young *Diplodocus,* separating it from the rest of its herd.

Wolf pack

Were any dinosaurs cannibals?

Fossil remains of *Coelophysis* found in New Mexico, United States, had skeletons of young ones inside them. The bones were too big to belong to unborn *Coelophysis*. Experts believe that adult *Coelophysis* would eat young of their own kind if food was short. Other dinosaurs may have been cannibals, too.

Did dinosaurs eat eggs?

Small speedy meat-eaters such as *Troodon* would snatch unguarded eggs from other dinosaurs' nests. Eggs were a good source of food — a complete meal in a shell! *Troodon* could sprint at about 50 kilometres an hour, so few lumbering plant-eaters could catch it.

The Fiercest Dinosaur

Tyrannosaurus rex ('king tyrant lizard') lived about 70 million years ago. At over 12 metres long and three times as tall as a man, it was one of the largest and deadliest creatures that has ever lived on land.

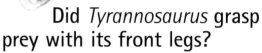

Has a whole *Tyrannosaurus* skeleton ever been found?

Complete fossil skeletons are very rare, but in 1990 two almost complete *Tyrannosaurus* skeletons were found in America. Experts studying these and other *Tyrannosaurus* skeletons believe that, unlike meat-eaters of today such as lions and tigers, the female *Tyrannosaurus* was probably bigger than the male.

Did *Tyrannosaurus* grasp prey with its front legs?

Tyrannosaurus' arms and hands were too small to grasp its prey. They couldn't even reach its mouth. Its head and teeth were so strong and deadly that it did not need its arms to catch its prey.

Tyrannosaurus skeleton

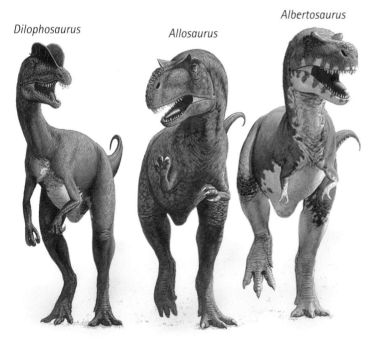

Dilophosaurus

Allosaurus

Albertosaurus

Were there other big meat-eaters?

These three meat-eaters were related to *Tyrannosaurus*, but were not as big. Two huge, 2.6-metre long fossil arms with clawed hands were found in Mongolia and named *Deinocheirus* ('terrible hand'). They may be from a version of *Deinonychus* that was even bigger than *Tyrannosaurus*.

How big were *T rex* teeth?

Tyrannosaurus had teeth up to 18 centimetres long. These teeth had a razor-sharp point to stab prey, and rough, saw-like edges to rip through flesh. An adult had between 50 and 100 teeth and if one fell out, it simply grew another!

Quick-fire Quiz

1. How long ago did *Tyrannosaurus* live?
   a) 200 million years
   b) 70 million years
   c) 150 million years

2. How long were its teeth?
   a) Up to 5cm
   b) Up to 30cm
   c) Up to 18cm

3. Which dinosaur was related to *Tyrannosaurus*?
   a) *Triceratops*
   b) *Albertosaurus*
   c) *Deinocheirus*

4. What does *Tyrannosaurus rex* mean?
   a) Big bad lizard
   b) King tyrant lizard
   c) Emperor reptile

Was *Tyrannosaurus* fast or slow?

Experts used to think that *Tyrannosaurus* stood upright and lumbered along, dragging its tail on the ground. By studying the more complete skeletons, they now think it leaned forward, with its tail sticking out as a balance, and that it could run fast. Judging from its skull and the size of its brain, experts think it also had good eyesight and hearing and an excellent sense of smell.

Wrong   Right

Was the fiercest dinosaur a scavenger?

Some experts think *Tyrannosaurus* was a scavenger that ate dead animals and stole prey from other predators. Others think it could run as fast as a racehorse (50 kilometres an hour) and was a fierce hunter. The latest finds show it probably did both.

Attack and Defence

Meat-eating dinosaurs were built to kill, attacking their victims with sharp teeth and slashing claws. Plant-eaters defended themselves in many different ways. Some lived in herds, some relied on speed to escape, while others developed armour and horns for fighting off enemies.

Did huge sauropods fight?

Like elephants today, the giant sauropods mostly relied on their size to protect them. Some, like *Diplodocus*, could lash their long, whip-like tails to frighten off attackers.

Which dinosaurs had armour?

Plant-eating ankylosaurs protected themselves with armour-like skin and bony spikes. *Ankylosaurus* was the size of a tank. If attacked, it crouched down to protect its soft belly and lashed out with the bony club on the end of its tail.

What use were plates and spikes?

Stegosaurus was well protected from its enemies with huge bony plates along its back and four long, sharp spikes on its thick tail. A blow from its tail could seriously injure, or even kill, an attacker.

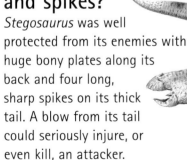

Armour or radiators?

The plates along the back of *Stegosaurus* were covered with skin and had lots of blood vessels in them. Some experts think they may have helped the dinosaur warm its body when it basked in the sun, and to cool down by losing heat quickly in the shade. Other scientists think the plates were armour to protect it from carnosaurs (meat-eating dinosaurs such as *Tyrannosaurus*).

Did plant-eaters have claws?

Most didn't but the plant-eater *Iguanodon* had two sharp thumb spikes. Perhaps it used them to stab attackers. Or maybe the males used them to fight each other.

Which dinosaurs had horns?

Some plant-eating dinosaurs, called ceratopians, developed horns and bony frills to protect themselves. They may have charged at enemies like a rhinoceros, or maybe rival males fought by locking horns.

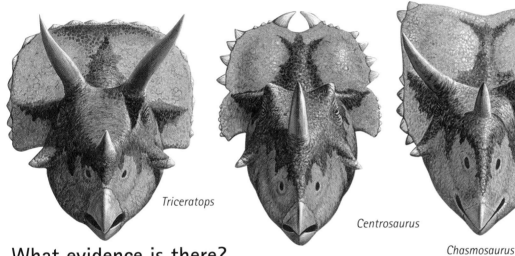

Triceratops

Centrosaurus

Chasmosaurus

Quick-fire Quiz

1. Which dinosaur had plates and spikes?
   a) *Stegosaurus*
   b) *Diplodocus*
   c) *Tyrannosaurus*

2. Which dinosaur had a tail club?
   a) *Velociraptor*
   b) *Ankylosaurus*
   c) *Diplodocus*

3. How did *Iguanodon* protect itself?
   a) With armour
   b) With thumb spikes
   c) With its horns

4. Which dinosaur died fighting with a *Velociraptor*?
   a) *Diplodocus*
   b) *Stegosaurus*
   c) *Protoceratops*

What evidence is there?

An amazing fossil was dug up in Mongolia in 1971. A *Protoceratops* had charged a fierce *Velociraptor* like a rhino, smashing into it with its bony beak. The *Velociraptor's* sharp claws had pierced the stomach and throat of the *Protoceratops*. Neither survived.

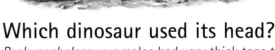

Which dinosaur used its head?

Pachycephalosaurus males had very thick tops to their skulls. Rival males may have had head-butting contests to win a mate, just as some wild sheep do today.

65

All Over the World

Stegosaurus

Maiasaura

Deinonychus

Diplodocus

This map shows where dinosaur fossils have been found. Experts have divided the dinosaur age into three main parts – the Triassic, Jurassic and Cretaceous Periods. Different dinosaurs lived in each of these periods, so some fossils are older than others.

What dinosaurs have been found in North America?

Hundreds of fossil dinosaurs, including *Diplodocus*, *Deinonychus* and *Stegosaurus*, have been found in North America. The famous *Tyrannosaurus* and *Triceratops* have been found only there, and nowhere else.

Cretaceous

Jurassic

Triassic

What was the fiercest dinosaur in South America?

The biggest South American meat-eater found so far is *Piatnitzkysaurus*, which was about 6 metres long and 3 metres high. It chased and killed prey in the same way as its bigger North American relative, *Allosaurus*.

Piatnitzkysaurus

Did some dinosaurs live all over the world?

Some dinosaurs, such as *Brachiosaurus*, have been found in North America, Africa and Europe. Other dinosaurs have only been found on one continent.

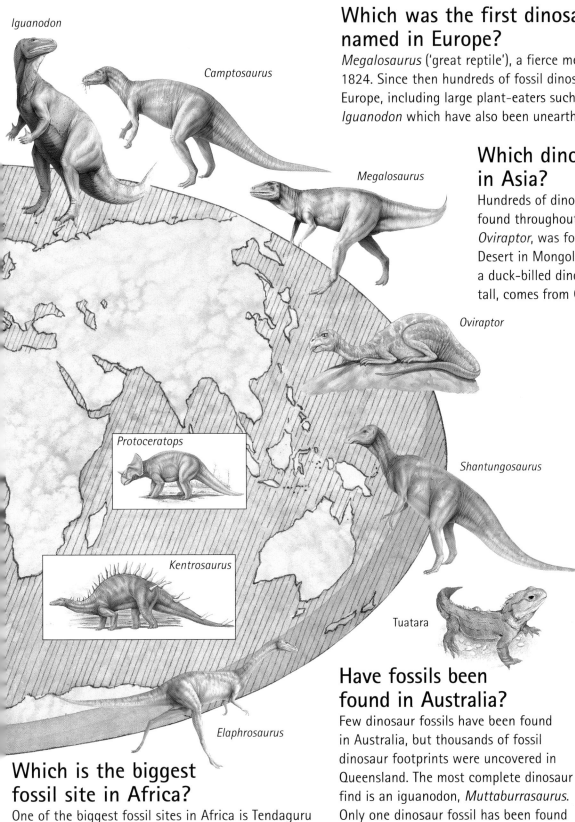

Iguanodon

Camptosaurus

Megalosaurus

Oviraptor

Protoceratops

Shantungosaurus

Kentrosaurus

Tuatara

Elaphrosaurus

Which was the first dinosaur to be named in Europe?

Megalosaurus ('great reptile'), a fierce meat-eater, was named in 1824. Since then hundreds of fossil dinosaurs have been found in Europe, including large plant-eaters such as *Camptosaurus* and *Iguanodon* which have also been unearthed in North America.

Which dinosaurs lived in Asia?

Hundreds of dinosaur remains have been found throughout Asia. The wolf-sized *Oviraptor*, was found in the remote Gobi Desert in Mongolia. *Shantungosaurus*, a duck-billed dinosaur about 12 metres tall, comes from China.

Which is the biggest fossil site in Africa?

One of the biggest fossil sites in Africa is Tendaguru in Tanzania. Over 200 tonnes of dinosaur bones were found there between 1909 and 1912. Many dinosaurs were dug up, including the stegosaur *Kentrosaurus* and the small bird-like *Elaphrosaurus*.

Have fossils been found in Australia?

Few dinosaur fossils have been found in Australia, but thousands of fossil dinosaur footprints were uncovered in Queensland. The most complete dinosaur find is an iguanodon, *Muttaburrasaurus*. Only one dinosaur fossil has been found in New Zealand, but the tuatara, a reptile that lives there today, looks almost exactly the same as its ancestors that lived in the dinosaur age.

Living in Herds

Clues, such as footprints and the mass dinosaur graves, show that some dinosaurs lived in groups. Plant-eating dinosaurs probably herded together for safety, like antelopes do today. Some meat-eaters may have hunted in packs.

Which dinosaurs probably lived alone?

Large meat-eating dinosaurs such as *Albertosaurus* were excellent hunters and had few enemies. They could have lived and hunted alone, just as tigers do today. However, the bones of 40 young and adult *Allosaurus* were discovered in a mass grave in the United States, so perhaps they hunted in packs like lions.

Why did dinosaurs live together?

Many plant-eaters like these *Edmontosaurus* hadrosaurs lived in herds for protection. Lots of pairs of eyes keeping watch for a predator are better than one pair. It is also more difficult for a predator to attack a large moving herd. These hadrosaurs probably hooted and honked to signal to each other if there was danger, such as a carnosaur, nearby.

Did herd members look after each other?

Fossil footprints show some dinosaur herds travelled with their young in the middle and the adults on the outside. If attacked, horned dinosaurs like *Triceratops* may have formed a circle round their young, with their horns pointing out towards the enemy, as musk oxen do today.

How do we know about dinosaur herds?

Vast tracks of fossilized dinosaur footprints all going the same way were discovered in North America. Experts believe they belonged to herds of dinosaurs. Huge numbers of dinosaurs have also been found buried together. One of these burial sites contained 10,000 duck-billed *Maiasaura*. This evidence shows sauropods probably lived in groups.

Why did some herds die together?

In 1947, the fossil remains of a large herd of *Coelophysis* were found at Ghost Ranch in New Mexico in the United States. The bones came from young and old animals. Some experts think they probably all died together in a flash flood. Their bodies were carried along by the water and eventually dumped in a heap on a sandbank where they fossilized.

Quick-fire Quiz

1. Where were a fossilized herd of *Coelophysis* found?
a) Ghost Ranch
b) Ghost Valley
c) Mexico Ranch

2. Which meat-eating dinosaur was found in a mass grave?
a) *Tyrannosaurus*
b) *Allosaurus*
c) *Diplodocus*

3. Why did *Edmontosaurus* herd together?
a) For company
b) For protection
c) To hunt

4. How many *Maiasaura* were found in a mass grave?
a) 40
b) 1,000
c) 10,000

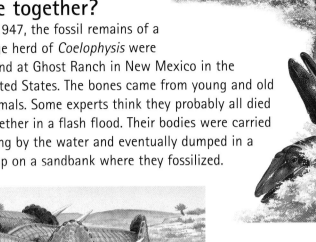

Did herds migrate?

Fossil dinosaurs have been found in the Arctic and Antarctic. There would have been plenty of food in the summer but little in winter. Experts think that dinosaur herds migrated away from the Poles in the winter, as modern-day caribou do.

Did dinosaurs travel far?

Like many animals today, such as caribou and wildebeest, some dinosaurs, such as these iguanodons, probably travelled huge distances in search of food.

Did dinosaur herds have look outs?

No-one knows for sure, but in large herds of animals some adults keep watch for predators. Dinosaurs probably did the same.

Which dinosaurs hunted in packs?

Carnivores like wolves and hyenas hunt in packs. Many small meat-eating dinosaurs, such as *Elaphrosaurus*, probably hunted in packs too. This would have allowed them to hunt and kill larger prey than if they hunted alone.

Fast and Slow

A dinosaur's shape, size, and the speed at which it moved, was determined by how it lived. Hunters had to be fast to catch their prey. They ran on strong back legs, using their tails to balance. Huge plant-eaters could only move slowly. They did not need to chase food and their huge size kept them safe.

Iguanodon

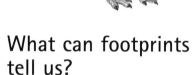

Megalosaurus

How can we measure a dinosaur's speed?

Experts work out the speed a dinosaur moved from the space between its footprints and the length of its legs. The wider apart a dinosaur's tracks are, the faster it was moving. If the footprints are close together, it was probably walking slowly.

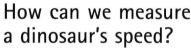

What can footprints tell us?

Fossilized footprints can show how dinosaurs moved. *Iguanodon* walked on all fours, but could run on its back legs. The huge three-toed prints of *Megalosaurus* show that it was a meat-eater and always moved on its back legs.

Which was the fastest dinosaur?

Ostrich-sized *Struthiomimus* was one of the fastest. It had no armour or horns to protect it and had to rely on speed to escape. It was as fast as a racehorse, reaching speeds of over 50 kilometres an hour.

How fast did dinosaurs move?

1 Just like animals today, dinosaurs moved at different speeds at different times. *Tyrannosaurus* walked at 16 kilometres an hour but ran much faster when attacking.

2 *Hypsilophodon* was one of the speediest dinosaurs. This plant-eater could race along the ground at up to 50 kilometres an hour to escape from enemies.

3 *Apatosaurus* weighed 40 tonnes — as much as seven elephants. It walked at 10 to 16 kilometres an hour. If it had tried to run, the impact would have broken its legs.

4 *Triceratops* weighed as much as five rhinos and could also charge like a rhino at speeds of over 25 kilometres an hour. Few predators would risk attacking it.

Which was the slowest dinosaur?

The huge sauropods like *Brachiosaurus* were the slowest moving dinosaurs. At over 50 tonnes, they were too heavy to run and so plodded along at about 10 kilometres an hour. Unlike smaller dinosaurs, these huge creatures were probably too big ever to have reared up on their hind legs.

Warm or cold blood?

Mammals and birds are warm-blooded — they make their own body heat. Reptiles are cold-blooded and have to warm up in the sun. To give them the energy to heat their bodies, warm-blooded animals need about ten times more food than a cold-blooded animal of the same size. Studying how much dinosaurs ate may show if any were warm-blooded.

In the Sea

While dinosaurs ruled the land, other giant reptiles took over the seas. Mosasaurs, plesiosaurs and pliosaurs were fierce predators, snapping up fish and other sea creatures. Giant turtles and crocodiles also hunted in prehistoric oceans.

Are all prehistoric sea reptiles extinct?

Most kinds of large sea reptiles died out with the dinosaurs, but turtles and crocodiles still exist. Prehistoric *Deinosuchus*, a 16-metre long crocodile, was, however, much bigger than any crocodile living today.

Deinosuchus

Kronosaurus

Mosasaurus

Teleosaurus

What did sea reptiles eat?

Sea reptiles ate fish, shellfish and even each other! A *placodont* picked up shellfish with its long front teeth. It crushed them with its back teeth, spat out the shells and swallowed the rest.

Ammonite (swimming shellfish)

Placodont

Why is Mary Anning famous?

Mary Anning was born in 1799 in Dorset, England. She grew up to be a great fossil hunter and was so good that she earned her living by selling fossils. She found the first complete fossil skeleton of a giant marine ichthyosaur when she was only 12 years old. Another of her amazing finds was the first complete skeleton of a plesiosaur.

Elasmosaurus

Tanystropheus

Did sea reptiles have teeth?

Most sea reptiles had large jaws full of sharp teeth to spear slippery fish or break open tough shells.

Ichthyosaurus

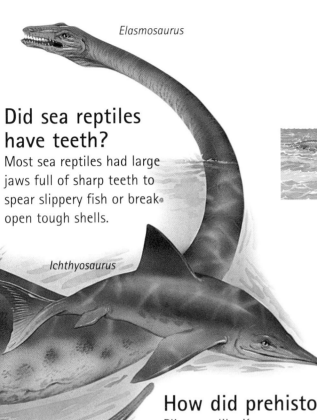

Did any sea creatures come on to the land?

Long-necked *Tanystropheus* hunted on both land and in the sea. It snapped up flying insects as well as slippery fish. Most sea reptiles had to come on land to lay their eggs.

How did prehistoric sea reptiles swim?

Pliosaurs like Kronosaurus and plesiosaurs like Elasmosaurus had four strong paddles instead of feet. They moved them up and down to 'fly' through the sea in the same way penguins do today. Mosasaurus, Ichthyosaurus and crocodiles such as Teleosaurus swam by beating their tails from side to side. Sea reptiles could not breathe under water, so they had to come to the surface to gulp in air.

Quick-fire Quiz

1. What was *Deinosuchus*?
a) A fish
b) A pliosaur
c) A crocodile

2. How did sea reptiles breathe?
a) At the surface
b) Under water
c) They didn't breathe air at all

3. Who found the first complete fossil Ichthyosaur?
a) Mary Mantell
b) William Buckland
c) Mary Anning

4. Which sea reptile gave birth to live young?
a) *Elasmosaurus*
b) *Ichthyosaurus*
c) *Archelon*

Kronosaurus skeleton

How big were the sea reptiles?

One of the biggest sea reptiles was the pliosaur *Kronosaurus*. It was nearly 17 metres long with a huge head the size of a car. *Mosasaurus* was 10 metres long, the largest lizard ever. Prehistoric turtles were much bigger than their modern relatives. The largest, *Archelon*, was almost 4 metres long. Its huge front paddles powered it through the water at up to 15 kilometres an hour.

Archelon

Did sea reptiles lay eggs?

Most sea reptiles laid their eggs on land, like turtles today. But *Ichthyosaurus* gave birth to live young in the same way as sea mammals like this dolphin do today.

73

In the Air

When dinosaurs took over the land, other reptiles took to the air. The first reptiles to become masters of flight were the pterosaurs. They ruled the skies for 166 million years but died out at the end of the dinosaur age.

How big were pterosaurs?

Pterosaurs came in many sizes. *Quetzalcoatlus* was the biggest. It had a human-sized body and a wingspan of over 12 metres — bigger than a hang glider! *Rhamphorhynchus* was the size of a crow with a wingspan of 40 centimetres.

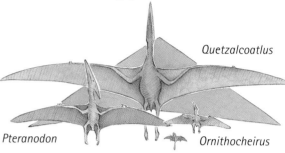

Quetzalcoatlus

Pteranodon

Ornithocheirus

Rhamphorhynchus

What did pterosaurs eat?

Pterosaurs' jaws and teeth help show what they ate. Most fed on fish, while some snapped up insects. *Pterodaustro* may have filtered tiny animals from the water with its sieve-like bottom jaw. *Dzungaripterus'* pincer-like beak could prise shellfish from rocks. *Dimorphodon's* strong jaws were ideal for catching fish.

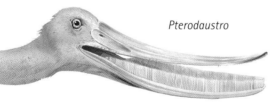

Pterodaustro

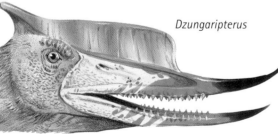

Dzungaripterus

Pteranodon

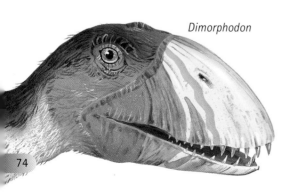

Dimorphodon

Did pterosaurs build nests?

No-one knows, but scientists think pterosaurs probably laid eggs. They may have laid these in nests, and sat on them to keep them warm. Fossils show that baby pterosaurs were not well developed, so perhaps the adults fed them, as baby birds are fed today.

Furry and active?

Fossil evidence shows that some pterosaurs were covered with fur, which probably means they were warm-blooded like birds. They also had big brains with large areas to control balance and sight.

74

When did reptiles first fly?

Reptiles first took to the air about 250 million years ago. Early flying reptiles, such as *Coelurosauravus*, were lizard-shaped with four legs. Their wings grew out from the sides of their body and were held rigid on long ribs. These reptiles used their wings to help them glide from tree to tree, but they could not flap them. One of the earliest gliding reptiles, *Longisquama*, had tall crests along its back. The crests may have opened out like wings to help it glide.

Longisquama

Coelurosauravus

Quetzalcoatlus

Bat

Did pterosaurs have tails?

All pterosaurs had tails. Early kinds, such as *Dimorphodon*, had long tails to increase lift and help them steer. Later types, such as *Pteranodon*, were called pterodactyls. They had much bigger wings and tiny tails.

Did pterosaurs have feathers?

Most pterosaurs had furry not feathered bodies and their wings were made from sheets of leathery skin. In this way, they were more like bats than birds. The wings stretched from the pterosaur's body along its arm to the tips of its long fourth fingers. Their long wings were ideal for soaring on air currents.

Death of the Dinosaurs

Dinosaurs died out about 65 million years ago. Studies show that they disappeared slowly in some places, but more suddenly in others. There are many theories to explain their death, but no-one knows for sure which is right.

Did a meteorite hit Earth?

One of the main theories is that a huge rock falling from outer space hit the Earth. This meteorite threw up a cloud of dust, blocking out the Sun's light and heat. The Earth became much colder and animals that could not cope with this died out. A huge crater that probably formed around this time has been found off the coast of Mexico. This evidence could mean that a meteorite caused the end of the dinosaurs.

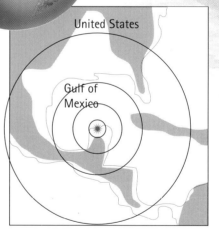

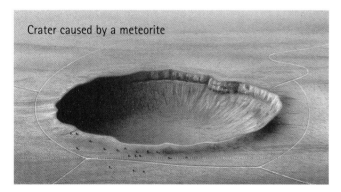

Crater caused by a meteorite

United States

Gulf of Mexico

※ Impact site

Did mammals eat dinosaur eggs?

One explanation for the death of the dinosaurs is that the number of small mammals increased. The mammals ate so many dinosaur eggs that few babies hatched. There are many strange theories and this is one of the more unlikely ones.

Did plant life change?

The extinction of dinosaurs and other animals may have been gradual. Towards the end of the dinosaur age, the tropical climate in North America became cooler and more seasonal and tropical plants were replaced by woodland plants. The dinosaurs seem to have migrated south, so perhaps they could not adapt to these changes in climate and plant life.

Did volcanoes make a difference?

Fossil plant remains suggest that by 65 million years ago the Earth's climate had become cooler. Some scientists think this was caused by several huge volcanic eruptions that took place over a period of half a million years. Volcanoes send up gases and dust that can first heat the atmosphere, then cool it down, killing off life.

Quick-fire Quiz

1. How long ago did dinosaurs die out?
a) 650 million years
b) 6 million years
c) 65 million years

2. Which other animals died out?
a) Pterosaurs
b) Mammals
c) Birds

3. Where was a huge meteorite crater found?
a) Europe
b) Mexico
c) Africa

4. Which of these reptiles survived?
a) Plesiosaurs
b) Turtles
c) Pterosaurs

Were there other mass extinctions?

The end of the dinosaurs was not the first mass extinction. About 440 million years ago almost half of the animal species died out, and again 370 million years ago. Over 95 per cent of all living things died out about 345 million years ago, and 210 million years ago, at the end of the Permian Period, many land vertebrates died out. When these events happen, new species can take over the world.

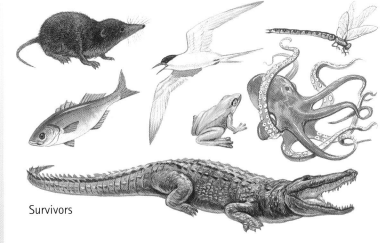

Survivors

Which animals died with the dinosaurs?

When the dinosaurs died out, so did many other reptiles, including mosasaurs, plesiosaurs, pliosaurs and pterosaurs. So did swimming shellfish like ammonites. Most other plants and animals, such as mammals, birds, frogs, fish and other kinds of shellfish survived. Not all reptiles died out either: turtles, crocodiles, snakes and lizards still exist today.

Timescale

The Earth formed about 4,600 million years ago and life developed about 1,000 million years later. The oldest known fossils, which are of shellfish, are 600 million years old. Dinosaurs arrived 230 million years ago and the first true humans about two million years ago.

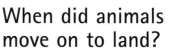

First life: 3,500 million years ago

Triassic

When did dinosaurs live?

The dinosaur age, the Mesozoic Era, lasted from 250 to 65 million years ago. Scientists split this time into three main periods. Dinosaurs first appeared in the **Triassic**, about 230 million years ago. The continents were a single land mass called Pangaea ('All-Earth') and dinosaurs could roam all over the world at that time. During the **Jurassic**, about 145 million years ago, Europe and Africa began to move away from the Americas. In the **Cretaceous**, the land masses were separated and different dinosaurs developed on the different continents.

When did animals move on to land?

Life began in the sea. The first animals moved on to land about 380 million years ago. Amphibians like Eryops could breathe air but, like frogs and toads today, they had to return to water to lay their eggs and to keep their skin moist. Eryops was the size of a pig. Its thick skin protected it and helped support its body weight on land.

DEVONIAN

CARBONIFEROUS

Eryops

Early Jurassic

Early Cretaceous

Tadpoles

Reptile hatching

Which animals first lived on land?

Although amphibians could live on land they were not true land animals as they had to return to the water to breed. The tiny tadpoles that hatched had to stay in the water until they developed into adults. Reptiles were the first vertebrates (animals with backbones) that could live completely on land. They laid their leathery eggs on land and the baby developed inside the egg, feeding on the yolk. The newly hatched baby was fully formed and active.

When did fish develop?

The first fish swam in the seas about 500 million years ago. None of them had jaws or fins. Later fish like *Dunkleosteus* were huge predators. This armoured giant was 10 metres long and its jaws were lined with razor-sharp bony cutters for slicing up prey. It lived 370 million years ago.

CAMBRIAN

Fish evolve: 500 million years ago

PRECAMBRIAN

Dunkleosteus

Modern times

Ornithomimus

TERTIARY

Hylonomus

Cetiosaurus

CRETACEOUS

TRIASSIC

JURASSIC

PERMIAN

Pentaceratops

The Mesozoic Era – the Age of the Dinosaurs

Eoraptor

Dimetrodon

Coelophysis

When did reptiles evolve?

Reptiles evolved about 320 million years ago. Early reptiles came in all shapes and sizes from the tiny *Hylonomus* at 20 centimetres long to 3 metres long *Dimetrodon*. One group of these early reptiles gave rise to the dinosaurs. Two of the earliest dinosaurs were *Eoraptor* and *Coelophysis*. Scientists think that another group of reptiles, called cynodonts, were the ancestors of mammals. Reptiles alive today include lizards, snakes, crocodiles, turtles and tortoises.

Quick-fire Quiz

1. What was the Age of Dinosaurs called?
a) Devonian
b) Mesozoic
c) Triassic

2. What was *Dunkleosteus*?
a) An amphibian
b) A reptile
c) A fish

3. What was the Triassic single land mass called?
a) Europe
b) Gondwana
c) Pangaea

4. What was *Dimetrodon*?
a) A dinosaur
b) A mammal-like reptile
c) An amphibian

79

After the Dinosaurs

After the dinosaurs died out, other animals developed to take their place. Warm-blooded mammals took over as the ruling animals. They dominated the land and even took to the air. A few even went to live in the place where life first developed – the sea.

What are the dinosaurs nearest surviving relatives?

Many scientists now agree that birds are the closest living relatives of the dinosaurs. The first fossil bird to be found was *Archaeopteryx*. It had a reptile-like skeleton similar to that of *Deinonychus* and feathered wings like a bird. *Archaeopteryx* had a long bony tail, three clawed fingers on each hand, and teeth. Modern birds have lost their teeth and their clawed wing fingers. Their small tail stumps hold their tail feathers.

Deinonychus

What were early birds like?

Very few fossils of early birds have been found. Several almost complete skeletons of *Hesperornis*, a diving bird that lived at the end of the dinosaur age, were found in the United States. *Hesperornis'* wings were so small that it was almost certainly flightless, but its large feet may have been webbed to help it swim. It looked much more like today's birds than *Archaeopteryx* but it still had teeth in its beak and a fairly long bony tail.

Why were mammals so successful?

There are several reasons. Early mammals had bigger brains and were more intelligent than reptiles. They were hairy and warm-blooded, so they could live in colder places. Most of them cared for their young for a long time, so perhaps more young survived. Also, different mammal groups had different kinds of teeth so they could feed on a huge range of food without competing with each other.

What were the first mammals like?

The first mammals evolved about 215 million years ago. One of the earliest known mammals is *Morganucodon*. This mouse-sized hunter was warm-blooded but probably laid eggs like the Australian platypus. *Zalambdalestes* lived at the same time as the last of the dinosaurs, and gave birth to live young.

Zalambdalestes

Morganucodon

Smilodon

When did mammoths die out?

The huge woolly mammoths died out about 10,000 years ago. The giant North American mammoth was as tall as a double-decker bus. These huge beasts were preyed on by *Smilodon*, a sabre-toothed cat with fangs as long as your hand (15 centimetres). When the mammoths died out, so did *Smilodon*.

Archaeopteryx

Pigeon

Mammoths

Late arrivals?

The first humans evolved about two million years ago, but modern humans or *Homo sapiens* ('wise person') only arose about 100,000 years ago. In the Stone Age, 20,000 years ago, people lived in caves and hunted with stone tools.

Quick-fire Quiz

1. Which of these have no teeth?
a) Birds today
b) *Archaeopteryx*
c) *Hesperornis*

2. Which was the earliest known mammal?
a) *Mammoth*
b) *Smilodon*
c) *Morganucodon*

3. How long ago did modern humans evolve?
a) 20,000 years
b) 100,000 years
c) 5,000,000 years

4. Which animals dominated after the dinosaurs?
a) Mammoths
b) Amphibians
c) Mammals

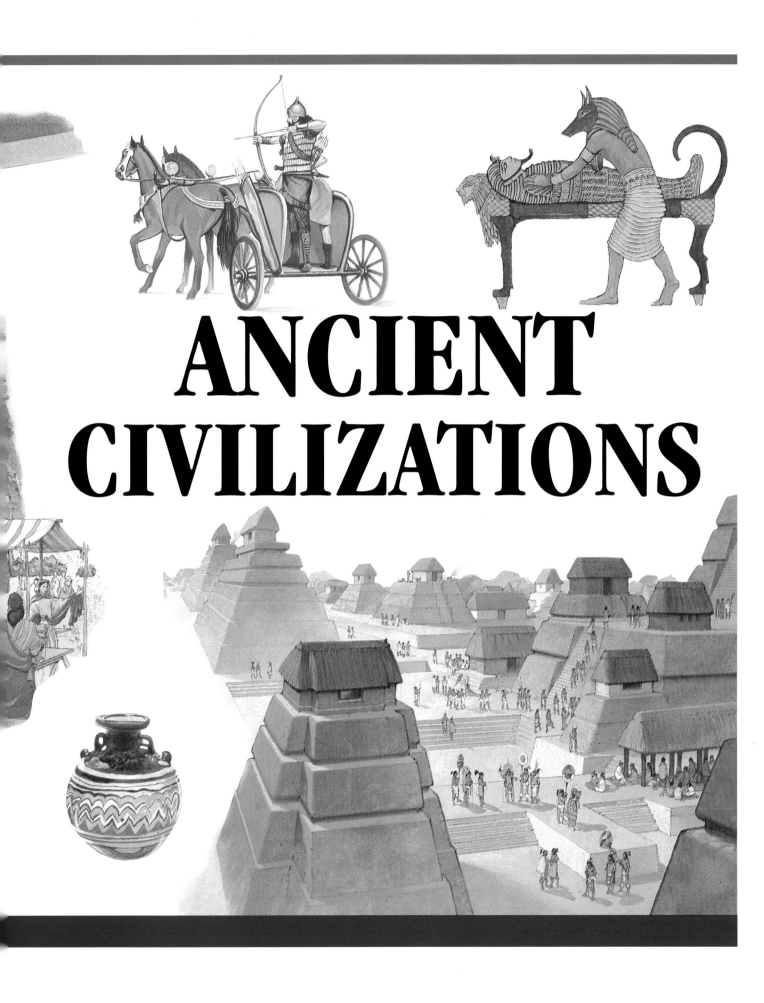

ANCIENT CIVILIZATIONS

The First Peoples

Early humans lived in caves and tents, moving from place to place in search of food. Around 8000 BC people began to grow crops and keep animals. These early farmers settled down and lived in small villages, which later grew larger and became towns and cities.

Who painted caves?

Over 100 cave paintings have been discovered in Europe, some dating back to about 25,000 BC. Rock paintings have been found in Africa and Australia. They were painted by prehistoric people, who used natural pigments to draw animals and hunting scenes.

Which was the largest ancient city?

The largest known ancient city is Çatal Hüyük in present-day Turkey. By 6250 BC, over 6,000 people lived there. The mud-brick houses were one storey high, but they did not have front doors. People entered by climbing a ladder and crawling through a hole in the roof.

What did the first people hunt?

Stone Age people hunted wild animals for food. One of the largest animals they hunted was the mammoth, a kind of prehistoric elephant. No part of a mammoth was wasted. The flesh fed a group of prehistoric people for weeks. Its furry skin was used to make clothes and tents, and the tusks and bones were used to build huts and carved to make jewellery.

What sort of gods did ancient people worship?

The early city-dwellers built religious shrines, but little is known about their gods. This clay figure, found at a decorated shrine in Çatal Hüyük, may have been a mother goddess.

Quick-fire Quiz

1. What was Çatal Hüyük?
a) A country
b) A kind of house
c) A city

2. What was a mammoth?
a) A prehistoric elephant
b) A prehistoric tiger
c) A prehistoric person

3. When were wolves tamed?
a) 2000 BC
b) 10,000 BC
c) 40,000 BC

4. What was made from palm leaves?
a) Rope
b) Paper
c) Bread

What did they eat?

People in Çatal Hüyük ate meat, fruits such as apples, and nuts and vegetables. They also made great use of date palms. They ate the fruit, the tree trunks provided timber, and the leaves were used to roof their houses or were plaited and woven into rope, mats and sandals.

Did the first people keep animals?

People tamed wolves as long ago as 10,000 BC. These were the first domesticated dogs and were used to herd other animals. In time, wild sheep, goats, cows and pigs were kept as farm animals.

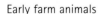

Early farm animals

What crops did they grow?

Early farmers sowed wild wheat and barley seeds. A new form of wheat with plumper seeds developed when wild wheat was cross-bred with a kind of grass. The farmers ground these seeds between stones, mixed the flour with water and made a new food — bread!

What were early villages like?

In Europe, the first villages were groups of houses in a fenced enclosure. The walls of the wooden houses were covered with mud, and the roofs thatched with dry grass. Vegetables were grown in one part of the enclosure, and farm animals were kept in another.

River Valley Civilizations

The first great civilization, Sumer, developed in about 5000 BC between the Tigris and Euphrates rivers. The area was later called Mesopotamia (now Iraq). Sumer lasted 3,000 years. In that time, other civilizations grew up along the River Nile in Egypt and the River Indus in Pakistan.

Did the Indus people build cities?

In the 1920s, two cities – Mohenjo-daro and Harappa – were found in the Indus valley. They dated from about 2000 BC, and were built in a grid pattern like modern American cities.

Who invented the wheel?

No-one knows when the wheel was invented. The potter's wheel was used in Mesopotamia about 6,000 years ago. By about 3200 BC the Sumerians were using simple carts like this. Later they had wheeled war chariots which were pulled by donkeys or wild asses.

Who invented writing?

Writing was probably invented by the Sumerians about 5,000 years ago. At first they drew pictures, but later these were turned into wedge-shaped symbols, which we now call cuneiform writing.

What crops did they grow?

Farmers in the Indus valley grew many crops, including wheat, barley, melons, dates and cotton. Each city had a huge, well-aired granary to store the grain between harvests.

Granary in Mohenjo-daro

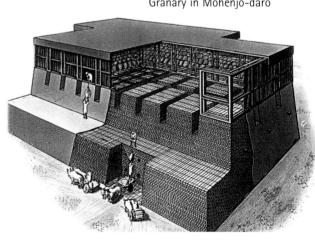

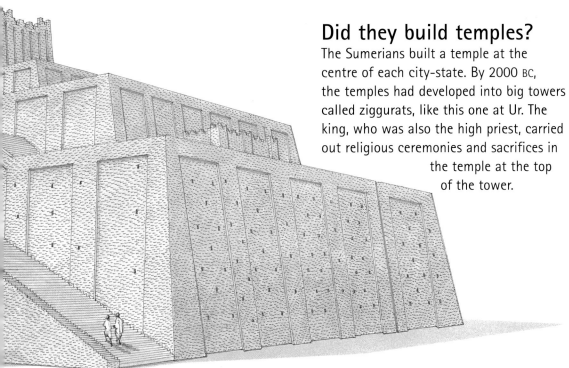

Did they build temples?

The Sumerians built a temple at the centre of each city-state. By 2000 BC, the temples had developed into big towers called ziggurats, like this one at Ur. The king, who was also the high priest, carried out religious ceremonies and sacrifices in the temple at the top of the tower.

Quick-fire Quiz

1. What was a ziggurat?
a) A house
b) A tower
c) A palace

2. What kind of writing did the Sumerians use?
a) Cuneiform
b) Hieroglyphs
c) Letters

3. Where was Harappa?
a) Sumer
b) Egypt
c) Indus valley

4. What did early Sumerians use to build their houses?
a) Wood
b) Stone
c) Reeds

What were river valley homes made from?

Most ancient peoples built homes from the materials around them. The Sumerians had no stones or trees, so they built houses from reeds and, later, sun-dried mud bricks. The Indus people lived in mud-brick houses built around courtyards. Each house had several rooms, a toilet and a well. The Indus civilization lasted 800 years. It came to an end in about 1800 BC.

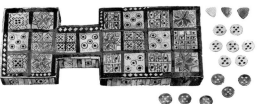

Did they play games?

Rich Sumerians did not have to work all the time, so they relaxed by listening to music or playing games. This game board, found in a royal grave at Ur, dates from between 3000 and 2000 BC. No-one knows how it was played.

Did the Sumerians have money?

The Sumerians traded at huge markets. Each trader had his own cylinder seal for signing contracts. Sales were recorded on clay tablets. By about 3300 BC, Sumerians were using clay tokens to buy goods. They may have had different sorts of tokens for different kinds of goods.

Who ruled Sumer?

Each Sumerian city-state had its own king. A king sometimes took over other cities, but none ever ruled all of Sumer. The royal families were very rich and wore fine clothes. A Sumerian princess wore a long dress with gold and silver jewellery.

87

Ancient Egypt

Over 5,000 years ago, two Egyptian kingdoms – Upper and Lower Egypt – grew up by the River Nile in North Africa. In 3100 BC, King Menes united Egypt. It became a very powerful empire which lasted until 30 BC, when Egypt fell to the Romans.

How do we know about ancient Egypt?

The remains of tombs, written records and wall paintings have helped build up a picture of ancient Egypt. Wall paintings show religious rituals, royal conquests and scenes of everyday life.

Did Egyptians play games?

Like most ancient peoples, wealthy Egyptians spent their leisure time listening to music or playing board games. Their children played with toys including balls, spinning tops, dolls and model animals.

Scribe

Who wrote letters?

Not all Egyptians could read and write. Men called scribes wrote letters for them. Scribes used hieroglyphs (picture writing) for royal and sacred writing, and simplified symbols for business letters. They used reed pens and a kind of paper called papyrus.

Did they wear wigs?

Yes, the ancient Egyptians thought that hair was dirty, so they shaved their heads and wore fancy wigs. They also wore make-up. They mixed powdered minerals such as lead, copper and iron oxide with water or oils to make bright lipstick, eye shadow and blusher.

How did Egyptians make bread?

Bread was the main food for poor Egyptians. Wheat and barley were ground into flour. They mixed this with water to make a dough, added flavouring such as garlic or honey, and baked it in clay pots.

Were pharaohs rich?

Egyptian kings, called pharaohs, were worshipped and treated like gods. They owned the whole country, and everybody and everything belonged to them, so they were very rich and powerful! The royal family lived in luxury, waited on by hundreds of servants.

Quick-fire Quiz

1. Who united Egypt?
   a) King Nile
   b) King Menes
   c) King Egypt

2. When did Egypt fall to the Romans?
   a) 300 BC
   b) 30 BC
   c) 3 BC

3. What did a scribe do?
   a) Make wigs
   b) Build tombs
   c) Write letters

4. What crop was swapped for goods?
   a) Peas
   b) Grain
   c) Garlic

Was grain used like money?

Grain was one of the most important crops in ancient Egypt. It was used to pay taxes, and was exchanged for other goods. For this reason, the Egyptians developed an accurate balance to weigh grain and other costly goods.

Why was the River Nile important?

The Egyptian empire grew up along the River Nile because it was good farming land. Hardly any rain fell in Egypt, but every July the River Nile flooded, covering the surrounding ground with water and rich black mud. This mud was great for growing crops. The ancient Egyptians learned how to store enough of the flood water in canals to irrigate (water) the fields in the dry season. This meant they produced enough crops to feed their own people and to sell some to other traders. Almost all Egypt's wealth came from farming.

Priests and Mummies

The ancient Egyptians worshipped many gods and believed in life after death. To make sure their spirits could enjoy the afterlife, the Egyptians embalmed (preserved) the bodies of the dead. The priests were very powerful, helping people with sacred works.

Why were tombs robbed?

Robbers plundered tombs for the treasures they contained. Rich Egyptians were buried with everything they would need in the afterlife – food, clothes, jewellery and even models of servants. Lucky amulets like these were often placed among a mummy's bandages to ward off evil spirits.

Who was mummified?

Making a mummy was expensive. Only the royal family, top officials and priests were mummified. The poor were buried in reed coffins or in holes in the sand. Animals that represented gods and goddesses, such as cats, dogs, crocodiles and baboons, were sometimes mummified. Cats, for example, represented the goddess Bastet.

What is a mummy?

A mummy is a body that has been preserved. The people who made mummies were called embalmers. After being dried out and rubbed with oils, the body was wrapped in bandages as much as five kilometres long! A priest watched over the embalmers as they worked.

Coffin

Embalmer

Priest

Amulets

Bandages

Canopic jars for the body organs

Which pharaoh's tomb survived?

Most pharaohs' tombs were robbed, but in 1922, archaeologists found the tomb of the young Tutankhamun, who was only 18 when he died. His tomb was still intact and full of priceless treasures, including his mummy and this fabulous golden face mask.

How was a body preserved?

The soft body organs were removed, dried, and placed in vessels called canopic jars. The spaces were packed with rags or sawdust, and the body was stitched up. It was then covered in a kind of salt called natron, which dried it out.

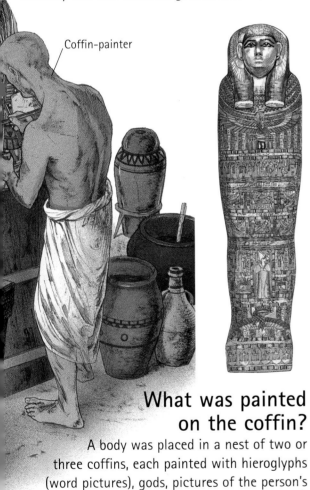

Coffin-painter

What was painted on the coffin?

A body was placed in a nest of two or three coffins, each painted with hieroglyphs (word pictures), gods, pictures of the person's life, and spells to keep away evil spirits.

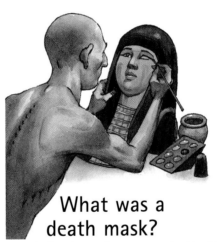

What was a death mask?

A death mask was a portrait of the dead person. It was put over the mummy's face, so that the soul would recognize its body. Death masks were often made of painted wood, but most pharaohs had death masks of beaten gold.

How was the brain removed?

An embalmer removed the brain by pulling it out through the nostrils with a hooked knife. They did not think the brain was important so they threw it away!

Who wore a jackal's head?

When the priest said the final prayers over a body, he wore a mask to look like the jackal god, Anubis, god of the dead. At the tomb, the priest held the mummy during the 'Opening of the mouth' ceremony, to give the dead person the power to eat, move and breathe.

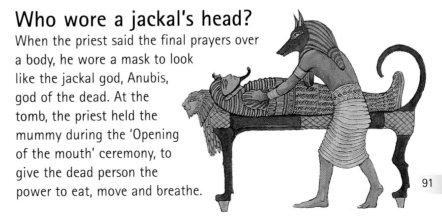

Pyramids and Tombs

Egyptian pharaohs of the Old and Middle Kingdoms (3,500 to 5,000 years ago), were buried under pyramids. In the New Kingdom (3,000 to 3,500 years ago), pharaohs were buried in tombs in a valley on the west bank of the Nile at Thebes.

How was a pyramid built?

It took at least 4,000 craftsmen and thousands of labourers to build a pyramid. The labourers were mostly farmers who worked as builders to pay their taxes. They cleared the site, laid the foundations and dragged the stones into place. Stone masons used an assortment of tools to cut the hard blocks of limestone used to cover the outside of the pyramids. They cut the stone into blocks that fitted together perfectly.

Plumb line

Chisels and hammers

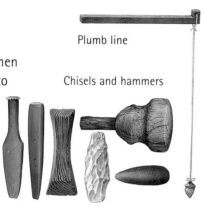

Stone masons

Which temple was moved?

In 1964, the temple at Abu Simbel was moved so that it would not be flooded when the Aswan dam was built. The temple had been carved out of solid rocks on the banks of the River Nile.

Why did Egyptians have funeral barges?

The mummified bodies of Egyptian pharaohs were placed on highly decorated boats so that they could travel to the next world. The boat was dragged to the tomb on a sledge pulled by oxen.

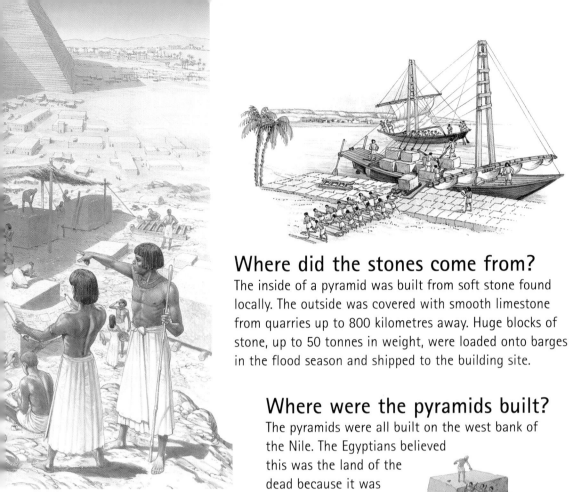

Where did the stones come from?

The inside of a pyramid was built from soft stone found locally. The outside was covered with smooth limestone from quarries up to 800 kilometres away. Huge blocks of stone, up to 50 tonnes in weight, were loaded onto barges in the flood season and shipped to the building site.

Where were the pyramids built?

The pyramids were all built on the west bank of the Nile. The Egyptians believed this was the land of the dead because it was where the Sun set. They built their homes on the east bank, the land of the living, where the Sun rose.

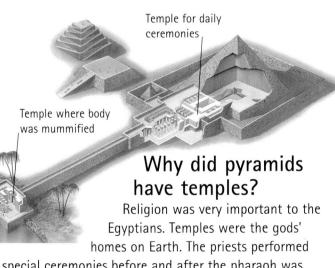

What is the Great Pyramid?

The Great Pyramid at Giza was built for King Khufu (c. 2575 BC) from over two million stone blocks. The pharaoh was buried in a central chamber.

Quick-fire Quiz

1. Where was the Great Pyramid?
a) Thebes
b) Giza
c) Abu Simbel

2. During which Kingdom were the pyramids built?
a) The Old Kingdom
b) All the time
c) The New Kingdom

3. What was built on the west bank of the Nile?
a) Egyptian homes
b) Pharaohs' palaces
c) The pyramids

4. When was the last pyramid built?
a) About 2575 BC
b) About 1570 BC
c) About 570 BC

Temple for daily ceremonies

Temple where body was mummified

Why did pyramids have temples?

Religion was very important to the Egyptians. Temples were the gods' homes on Earth. The priests performed special ceremonies before and after the pharaoh was put in the tomb, so temples were built in the pyramids.

Why did pyramid-building stop?

About 90 pyramids were built – the last one in 1570 BC. But they were easy for robbers to get into, so pharaohs of the New Kingdom were buried in tombs carved in the cliffs in a hidden valley at Thebes instead. This is known as the Valley of the Kings. Although most of these tombs were also robbed, it was here that archaeologists Howard Carter and Lord Carnarvon, found the untouched tomb of the boy-king, Tutankhamun.

Crete and Mycenae

The first European civilization began about 4,500 years ago, on the island of Crete. The Minoans, named after a famous king, Minos, were traders who ruled the Aegean Sea. In 1450 BC, this civilization ended and the Mycenaeans, from mainland Greece, took over.

What was the minotaur?

The Minoans told how King Minos kept a minotaur, a monster that was half-man and half-bull, in a labyrinth (maze of tunnels) below his palace. Each year, he sacrificed 14 young Greeks to this terrible creature. The Greek hero, Theseus, was determined to kill the minotaur. With the help of King Minos's daughter, Ariadne, he found a way into the labyrinth, killed the monster and escaped from the maze by following a thread he had unwound on his way through it.

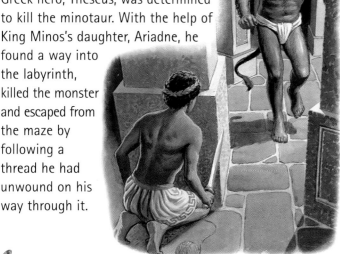

What goods did the Minoans trade?

Craftsmen made beautiful pottery and carved ornaments. Goldsmiths made fine jewellery, such as this bull's head pendant. Minoan goods have been found in many surrounding countries including Egypt.

Did Minoans build cities?

The Minoans built several cities, connected to each other by paved roads. Each had a fine palace. The grandest was at Knossos, in the north of Crete. It had over 1,000 rooms, including luxurious apartments, workshops and a school.

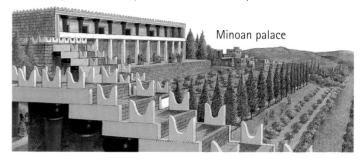

Minoan palace

Who went hunting?

The Mycenaeans loved to hunt wild animals, including lions, which roamed Greece until about 3,000 years ago. This fresco shows a boar hunt. Nobles hunted boar with spears and shields, and had dogs to help them. Hunters cut off the tusks from dead boars, and used them to decorate their helmets.

Did Minoans play sports?

Frescoes (wall-paintings) show the Minoans were very sporty. Boys and girls enjoyed boxing and the dangerous sport of bull-leaping. One person held the bull's head, while the bull-leaper somersaulted between the horns of the bull. A friend stood at the back to catch the acrobat.

What were Mycenaean palaces like?

The Mycenaeans were the ruling Greeks from about 1450 BC until 1100 BC. The remains of the palace of the Mycenaean king Nestor at Pylos, in southern Greece, show that it had richly decorated rooms built around a series of courtyards.

Mycenaean palace

The Lion Gate

Were the Mycenaeans warriors?

The Mycenaeans, unlike the Minoans, were warriors as well as traders, and built fortified towns. The walls around their city of Mycenae were built from huge stone blocks. At the only entrance, the Lion Gate, a pair of stone lionesses stood guard. Warriors attacked their enemies from the walls.

Quick-fire Quiz

1. Which of these civilizations began in Crete?
a) Egyptian
b) Mycenaean
c) Minoan

2. What was the minotaur?
a) Half-man, half-lion
b) Half man, half-bull
c) Half-man, half-boar

3. Who killed the minotaur?
a) King Minos
b) King Nestor
c) Theseus

4. What was the main gate in Mycenae called?
a) The Lion Gate
b) The Bull Gate
c) The King Gate

Babylon

The Mesopotamian city-state of Babylon rose to power in 1900 BC. Hammurabi the Great increased its power in the 1700s BC. It collapsed in 1595 BC, but grew great again under Nebuchadnezzar, 1,000 years later. In 539 BC, Babylon fell to the Persians.

Who made Babylon rich?

Nebuchadnezzar made Babylon one of the richest cities in the world. The main entrance, the Ishtar gate, was covered with glazed blue tiles. He brought plants and trees from Persia for the famous Hanging Gardens, which were one of the 'Seven Wonders of the Ancient World'.

Did the Babylonians go to war?

The Babylonian army was well trained and had good leaders. Both Hammurabi the Great and Nebuchadnezzar waged wars against surrounding lands. Skilled archers helped Nebuchadnezzar conquer lands, including Phoenicia, Syria, Judah and Assyria.

What were their houses like?

About 4,000 years ago, most people in Babylon had simple homes. However, rich people built large, flat-roofed houses with wooden balconies around a central courtyard. They lived in great comfort, with many servants to cook and clean for them.

Who lost the secret of eternal life?

Legend tells how the Babylonian hero and king, Gilgamesh, was given the secret of eternal life – a plant from under the sea. He dived and picked the plant but he fell asleep on his way home. A snake gobbled up the plant and Gilgamesh lost the chance to live forever.

Did they have gods?

The people of Babylon had many gods. Ishtar, the mother goddess, and Marduk, the dragon god, were the most powerful. One myth tells how the hero Gilgamesh's pride angered the gods, who sent a Bull of Heaven to destroy him – but Gilgamesh survived.

Quick-fire Quiz

1. Who was the mother goddess?
a) Marduk
b) Ishtar
c) Gilgamesh

2. How many laws did Hammurabi make?
a) 282
b) 272
c) 262

3. What ate the secret of life?
a) A snake
b) A bull
c) A genie

4. Who conquered Babylon in 539 BC?
a) The Greeks
b) The Egyptians
c) The Persians

What were genies?

The Babylonians believed that winged gods, or genies, protected royal palaces from demons and disease. This genie is holding a bucket and a pine cone, which were symbols of purification.

Who made good laws?

Hammurabi made 282 laws for his people to follow. Most were good laws, to protect the weak from the strong. They covered everything from fair rates of pay to rules for trading.

Did they keep pets?

Some Babylonians probably had domesticated cats and dogs, but rich people kept more exotic pets. The first zoos were owned by wealthy princes, who gave each other presents of wild animals such as lions and leopards.

Did Babylonians do maths?

Like earlier people in the region, the Babylonians used cuneiform writing, which can still be seen on clay tablets. Babylonian mathematicians worked out a system of counting based on the number 60. This was especially useful as 60 can be divided in many different ways. We still use this system today when we record the time (60 minutes in an hour, 60 seconds in a minute), and in measuring (there are 60 x 6 degrees in a circle). Babylonians recorded details of royal grants of land on boundary stones which deterred land disputes between neighbours. The Babylonians were also great astronomers.

Assyrians and Hittites

The Hittites from Anatolia (now in Turkey) conquered most of Syria, Mesopotamia and Babylon in the 1500s BC. Their empire fell in 1200 BC and the Assyrians, from northern Mesopotamia, took over. In 609 BC, the Assyrian empire fell to the Babylonians.

What did they build?

The Assyrians built magnificent cities, temples and palaces. The king often supervised the building from his chariot. Stones were brought from distant quarries, and oarsmen in skin boats towed laden rafts up the Tigris.

Who used battering rams?

Both the Hittites and the Assyrians were skilled at using siege warfare to defeat their enemies. Their armies would surround the enemy's city to stop food getting in. Then they used huge battering rams to knock holes in the city walls.

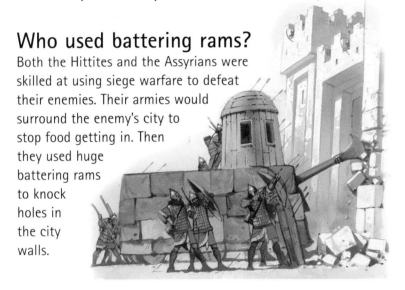

Who last ruled Assyria?

King Ashurbanipal was the last and greatest ruler of Assyria. He was a ruthless king, but he also built a great library where records and literature from Sumer and Babylon were stored on clay tablets. His palace at Nineveh had gardens stocked with plants from all over the world.

The Assyrian royal court

Who carved in stone?

The Hittites and Assyrians were great stone masons. The Hittites carved huge pictures of their gods and goddesses into the rock face near their temples. The Assyrians left many finely carved stone sculptures which tell us about their history and how they lived. Most of them show the kings and their conquests, but this one shows scenes of everyday life such as people preparing and cooking food.

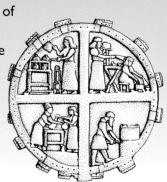

Carved stone being dragged to a new temple

Quick-fire Quiz

1. Who was Ashur?
a) A god
b) A king
c) A goddess

2. Where were the Hittites from?
a) Syria
b) Egypt
c) Anatolia

3. Where was Ashurbanipal's palace?
a) Babylon
b) Nineveh
c) Sumer

4. What animals pulled a war chariot?
a) Bulls
b) Lions
c) Horses

Winged lion

What gods did the Assyrians worship?

The Assyrians believed in many gods. Their chief god was Ashur whose name was used for their capital city. Ishtar was the Assyrians' goddess of war. The Babylonians also worshipped Ishtar, but believed that she was a mother-goddess who helped protect their city. To ward off evil spirits, huge stone sculptures of winged lions with human heads were placed on each side of important doors and gateways.

Who drove war chariots?

Both the Hittites and the Assyrians used war chariots in battle. The two-wheeled chariots were drawn by horses, and the skilled archers would fire at the enemy as they raced along. The Assyrians were fierce warriors, fighting with swords, slings, shields and bows.

Assyrian war chariot

Ancient Sea Traders

The Phoenicians were the best sea traders of the ancient world. They lived in city-states on the coast of the Mediterranean Sea (now Lebanon) from about 1200 to 146 BC. Their culture died out after the area was conquered by Alexander the Great.

Were the Phoenicians explorers?

The Phoenicians were skilled sailors and had fine ships. Around 600 BC, the Egyptians paid the Phoenicians to explore West Africa. They also sailed to Britain, where they traded goods for tin and silver.

What goods did Phoenicians trade?

Phoenician craftsmen made fine cloth as well as pottery, ivory and metal goods to sell. They also traded in the wood from cedar trees.

Who blew glass?

The Phoenicians were the first people to produce see-through glassware on a large scale. They also invented the process of glass blowing, which allowed them to make fine glassware like this.

Letters from the Phoenician alphabet

Could Phoenicians read and write?

The Phoenicians must have been able to read and write because they were among the first people to use an alphabet for writing words, rather than pictograms. Their alphabet was made up of 30 consonants — there were no vowels. These letters became the basis for all modern alphabets.

How did the Phoenicians get their name?

The name came from the Greek word 'phoinos' meaning 'red'. They were called this because they made a rich reddish-purple dye from a sea snail called a murex. Cloth dyed with this was expensive. In Roman times, only emperors were allowed to wear murex-dyed robes.

Murex

Who founded the city of Carthage?

Carthage was the largest Phoenician city. According to legend, the founder of Carthage was the Phoenician princess Dido. After landing on the coast of North Africa, Dido asked the local ruler for land to build a city. He said she could take an area of land that could be enclosed by an ox-hide. Clever Dido had the hide cut into thin strips so that she could mark out a large plot of land. Carthage became one of the most important trading cities in the area.

Did they build temples?

The Phoenicians built many temples and shrines to their gods. Their main god was the warrior god Baal. There were priests and priestesses, who occasionally, in times of trouble, sacrificed children to the gods.

Phoenician priestess

Where were Phoenician colonies?

The Phoenicians spread throughout the Mediterranean, setting up colonies in many foreign lands including Marseilles (France), Cadiz (Spain), Malta, Sicily, Cyprus and Carthage (now Tunisia) in North Africa. From Carthage they traded with local Africans, buying precious ivory, animal skins and wood.

Phoenicians trading with Africans

Ancient Greece

By 500 BC, ancient Greece was made up of small, independent city-states around the Mediterranean. Each city-state had its own government and laws. The most important of these city-states were Athens and Sparta.

Who were the Spartans?

The city-state of Sparta in southern Greece was a mighty military power. All Spartan men were in the army, and boys left home at seven to start training as soldiers. Women did not fight, but they had to be very fit so their babies would be healthy and strong.

What was an acropolis?

Each Greek city-state had a walled city with an acropolis (fort) and an agora — a large open space used for meetings and markets. In time the acropolis became a religious centre.

Who left Athens?

Criminals or unpopular politicians could be banished (ostracized). Each year, Athenians could write the name of a person they wanted banished on bits of pottery called 'ostraka'. Anyone with more than 6,000 votes had to leave for 10 years!

Did Greeks play sports?

The ancient Greeks enjoyed competitive games. The Olympics – the most famous – were first held in 776 BC, and took place every four years. At first, there was just one race. By 500 BC, the Games lasted five days.

Ancient Greek athletes competed naked

Who won an olive wreath?

On the final day of the Olympic Games the winners received their prizes – crowns of laurel leaves or wild olives cut from a special grove near the temple of Zeus. Afterwards they were guests of honour at a victory feast.

Who played outdoors?

Greek plays were performed in large open-air theatres. The semicircular theatre in Athens held over 10,000 people. All the actors were male, and they wore brightly painted masks to show which characters they were playing.

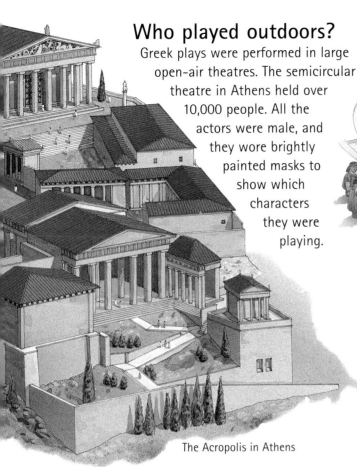

The Acropolis in Athens

Did they enjoy music?

The Greeks enjoyed singing and dancing, and music was played on most social occasions. Poetry was chanted, accompanied by music, or sung. The main stringed instrument was the lyre, which was sometimes made from a tortoise shell.

Who read the future?

The Greeks had many gods. The chief was Zeus who lived on Mount Olympus, the highest mountain in Greece. If the Greeks wanted to ask the gods about the future, they visited oracles. Priests and priestesses at an oracle spoke on behalf of the gods. The advice from the gods was usually so vague that it always seemed to be right. The most famous oracle was in the temple of the sun god, Apollo, at Delphi.

Consulting the oracle at Delphi

Whose speeches were timed?

In Athens, all men who were not slaves were citizens, and could speak at the Assembly. At this meeting they could give their opinions on political matters. Each speaker was timed with a water clock, so he could not talk for too long!

Quick-fire Quiz

1. What foretold the future?
a) The Assembly
b) An acropolis
c) An oracle

2. What was a lyre?
a) A bird
b) A musical instrument
c) An Olympic sport

3. How often were the Olympic Games held?
a) Every year
b) Every four years
c) Every ten years

4. Who could speak at the Assembly?
a) Citizens
b) Slaves
c) Everyone

Greek Life

Greek architecture, the arts, sport and science flourished during the Golden Age (600 to 300 BC). Athens became the centre of Greek culture. In 338 BC, King Philip of Macedonia conquered Greece. His son, Alexander the Great, spread Greek learning to North Africa and the Middle East.

Where did people shop?

In the agora, or marketplace, you could buy everything from food to fabrics, silverware to slaves. Fast-food sellers supplied tasty snacks, and you could even visit a doctor.

What were Greek houses like?

Greek houses were made of sun-dried, mud bricks built round a central courtyard. Most houses were single storey, but some wealthier homes had bedrooms on a second floor. Greek men, women and slaves all lived in separate quarters.

How do we know about ancient Greek life?

Archaeologists have found marble and bronze statues and pottery bowls, vases and cups decorated with scenes from Greek life. These tell us what the Greeks wore and how they lived.

What did ancient Greeks eat?

Basic foods were bread, olives, figs and goats' milk cheese. Meat was expensive but fish was cheap along the coast. Women prepared the food, and everyone ate in the courtyard.

What did Greeks wear?

Everyone wore a chiton – a large cloth rectangle fastened at the shoulders. Saffron yellow was a favourite colour, but purple, red and violet were also fashionable. Wealthy women piled their hair into elaborate styles, and wore make-up, earrings, necklaces, bracelets and rings.

104

Did Greeks have baths?

Few homes had baths, but the gymnasium, a public sports ground in Athens, had plunge pools and steam baths. Women and children washed using bronze basins, and some homes had terracotta hip baths. Slaves helped their masters to wash.

Where did people relax?

The agora was a place to relax and meet friends. Men met there to listen to storytellers recounting tales, or to hear philosophers such as Socrates discuss politics.

Quick-fire Quiz

1. What was an agora?
a) A school
b) A marketplace
c) A temple

2. Who went to school?
a) Boys
b) Girls
c) No-one

3. What was a chiton?
a) A stool
b) A book
c) A robe

4. Who conquered Greece in 338 BC?
a) Philip
b) Alexander
c) Socrates

Did they have furniture?

Wealthy Athenians lived in heated homes with fine furniture. They lounged on padded couches and ate from small tables inlaid with ivory. Their wooden beds had leather thongs to support a mattress, and lots of cushions.

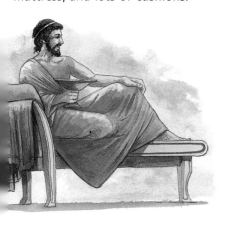

Did Greek children go to school?

Rich Athenian boys went to school between the ages of seven and 18. They studied maths, reading, writing, music and poetry in the morning and did athletics and dancing in the afternoon. The girls stayed at home, learning to spin, weave and run a household.

The Persians

About 3,000 years ago, Persia (Iran) was ruled by two powers, the Medes and the Persians. In 550 BC, Persian king, Cyrus the Great, seized power. He made Persia the centre of a huge empire, which lasted until 330 BC, when Alexander the Great took control.

Who was Alexander the Great?
Alexander the Great became king of Greece in 336 BC, and set out to conquer the Persians. He was a great soldier and a clever leader. Within 12 years he had taken over Persia, and built an empire stretching from Egypt to India.

Who made Persia great?
King Darius I ruled Persia from 521 to 486 BC. His powerful empire included Egypt and the Indus Valley. He taxed all the people he conquered, and the tributes they brought him included food, animals, fine cloth, gold and jewels. He built roads to link the empire, and introduced a standard currency to increase trade.

Who were the Parthians?

The Parthians moved into Persia in about 1000 BC and lived under Persian rule. After the death of Alexander the Great, the Parthians took over the area. A favourite trick of Parthian archers was to pretend to retreat, then turn in their saddles to fire back at the enemy – the origin of the saying 'a Parthian shot'.

What sort of religion did the Persians have?

Many Persians worshipped Mithras, the god of light, truth and justice. There was a legend that he killed a magic bull, and that every animal and plant sprang from its blood. Later, Mithras was popular with Roman soldiers, who built temples to him. A Persian prophet called Zoroaster, who lived around 600 BC, founded a new religion, Zoroastrianism, which is still followed today in parts of Iran and India.

Quick-fire Quiz

1. Who founded the Persian empire?
a) King Cyrus
b) King Darius
c) King Philip

2. When was the Battle of Salamis?
a) 380 BC
b) 480 BC
c) 580 BC

3. Who or what was Zoroaster?
a) A palace
b) A city
c) A prophet

4. What was a trireme?
a) A god
b) A sword
c) A ship

Did Persia have an army?

The Persians had a large, well-trained army. The soldiers were armed with spears, daggers and bows and arrows. They wore leather tunics strengthened with scales to protect them in battle.

Was Persia rich?

Persia became very rich under Darius I, who lived in a huge palace in Persepolis. The Great Hall alone held 10,000 people. When Alexander the Great invaded, he is said to have taken 4,500 tonnes of gold from the Persian cities of Persepolis and Susa.

Did the Persians and Greeks fight?

The Greeks and Persians were at war for many years. At the Battle of Salamis, in 480 BC, the Persian fleet was forced to retreat by the might of the Greek triremes. A trireme was a swift ship powered by more than 150 oarsmen grouped in threes on either side of the ship.

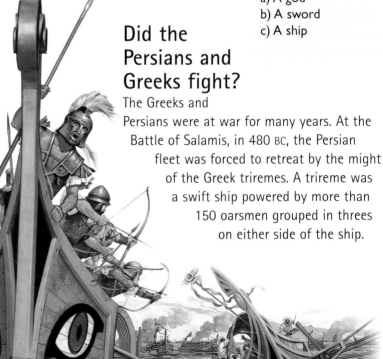

Ancient China

The first emperor of China was King Zheng of Qin. In 221 BC, he defeated the rulers of all the states that made up China, and founded the Qin dynasty, from which China gets its name. The Han dynasty (206 BC to AD 220) opened up trade with the West.

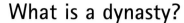

What is a dynasty?

China was governed by a series of ruling families, called dynasties. The Zhou dynasty ruled China for over 800 years from 1122 BC. Zhou society was divided into nobles, peasants and slaves. Iron was first used at this time, and farming methods improved.

Who was Confucius?

Confucius, or K'ung Fu-tzu, was born in China in 551 BC. He was a great thinker who believed that the emperor should care for his people like a father, and that the people should love and obey him. For over 2,000 years his teachings influenced the way China was ruled.

What was the terracotta army?

When King Zheng became emperor, he changed his name to Shi Huangdi ('first emperor') and ordered a splendid tomb to be built. His tomb was guarded by a terracotta army – 7,000 life-size clay soldiers. The soldiers had real crossbows and spears, with life-size clay horses and chariots.

Who invented paper?

Chinese inventors discovered many useful things. Around AD 100, a man called Tsai Lung rolled a paste of hemp and wood into a sheet which he stretched and dried. He had invented paper! About 800 years later, the Chinese printed the first banknotes.

What are Yin and Yang?

The Chinese believe everything in nature is in harmony. Confucius depicted this by the Yin and Yang symbol. The dark Yin interlocks with the light Yang, and each one contains a tiny bit of the other.

Who invented the compass?

The ancient Chinese were great scientists and inventors. During the Han dynasty, scientists invented the first magnetic compass with a dial and a pointer. At first, they did not use it for navigation, as we do now, but to make sure that their temples faced the right way. The Chinese were very skilled sailors. Hundreds of years before the Europeans, the Chinese built sea-going ships with lots of sails and steered by rudders. Chinese sailors travelled as far as Africa to trade. They were also skilled mathematicians and astronomers. The Chinese were the first to make maps using a grid system, and to work out that a year has 365.25 days.

Who built the Great Wall?

The Great Wall of China was built for Shi Huangdi between 214 and 204 BC, by thousands of poor farmers. Short bits of wall were joined up to make the longest wall in the world, stretching over 2,200 kilometres. The wall is up to 15 metres high, and is wide enough for a bus to drive along the top.

Who defeated an emperor?

Life was hard for most peasants during the Qin dynasty. They had to pay taxes and work for Shi Huangdi. After his death, the peasants rebelled against the new emperor, his son. They raised a large army and, in 209 BC, the emperor was defeated.

Peasants during the Qin Dynasty

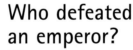

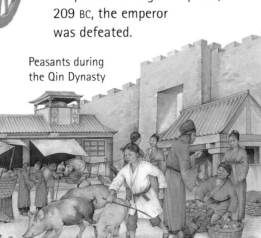

Quick-fire Quiz

1. What did the terracotta army guard?
a) A palace
b) A tomb
c) A city

2. Who invented paper?
a) K'ung Fu-tzu
b) Shi Huangdi
c) Tsai Lung

3. How high is the Great Wall?
a) 25m
b) 15m
c) 5m

4. When was Confucius born?
a) 551 BC
b) 151 BC
c) 51 BC

The Celts

Between 750 and 50 BC, the Celts were the most important tribes in Europe. There were many different Celtic tribes, but they all spoke the same kind of language and had similar lifestyles. Eventually, the Romans conquered most of their lands.

What were Celtic homes like?
A Celtic house often had walls made of branches covered with clay, and a thatched roof of straw or reeds. Most homes had one large room, where the family cooked, ate and slept. There were no windows. A central fire provided heat and light.

Were the Celts warriors?
Celtic men and women were renowned fighters and battles between tribes were common! Many warriors painted their faces and bodies blue to look as fierce as possible. Some went into battle naked but others wore tartan tops, capes and trousers, and carried fine bronze shields.

Were the Celts interested in arts and crafts?
The Celts were great poets and musicians and made beautifully decorated metalwork. Wealthy warriors carried fine shields, and often wore an armband made from gold and a delicately carved neck ring, called a torque. Celtic jewellery and weapons were decorated with abstract or geometrical designs.

Shield

Armband

Were cattle important?

The Celts were farmers. They depended on meat to get them through the winter, so cattle were very important. At the feast of Beltane on May 1, which marked the start of summer, Druids (priests) chased cattle through bonfires to expel evil spirits and disease.

A bull's head decoration from a cauldron found in Denmark

What are Celtic myths about?

Very few Celtic myths and stories have survived. Some of the best known come from Ireland and Wales. The Welsh Mabinogion tells the mythical history of early Britain. In this scene from an Irish myth, a giant brings a king a magic cauldron, which represents plenty, fertility and rebirth.

Quick-fire Quiz

1. What was a torque?
a) An earring
b) A neck ring
c) A belt

2. When was Beltane celebrated?
a) November
b) February
c) May

3. What was a Druid?
a) A priest
b) A warrior
c) A king

4. What is Stonehenge?
a) A feast
b) A city
c) A monument

Who built Stonehenge?

Stonehenge in England was built by Stone Age people in around 2750 BC, long before the Celts. The layout of the huge circle of standing stones marked the midsummer sunrise and the midwinter moonrise. Historians think this monument was used as a place of worship and to study the stars. Later, Celts may have used it as a meeting place for worship and to make sacrifices to their gods.

Could Celts read and write?

Celts did not read or write. Their myths, laws and religion were passed down by word of mouth. Druids taught poetry, history and the law. At feasts, musicians and storytellers called bards told tales of brave heroes.

Life in Ancient Rome

At first, ancient Rome was ruled by kings, but in 509 BC the Romans set up a republic with elected leaders. Rome gradually took over other lands, and by AD 150 the empire stretched across Europe into Africa.

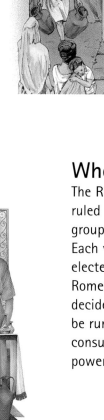

Who were looked after by wolves?

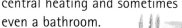

According to Roman legend, a king named Numitor had two baby grandsons, called Romulus and Remus. They were thrown into the River Tiber, but a wolf rescued them and brought them up. When they grew up, the brothers built Rome.

Where did rich Romans live?

Many rich Romans had a country home (a villa) and a town house (a domus). Houses were built around a courtyard and had lots of rooms, running water, a kitchen, central heating and sometimes even a bathroom.

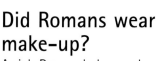

Did Romans wear make-up?

A rich Roman lady powdered her face with chalk or white lead and painted her lips with red ochre. She took a long time to get ready for the day, even though slave girls helped her dress and style her hair.

Who ruled Rome?

The Roman republic was ruled by the Senate – a group of elder citizens. Each year, the Senate elected two consuls to lead Rome. The Senate met to decide how Rome was to be run and to advise the consuls, who were the most powerful people in Rome.

Where did the poor live?

Romans with little money lived in tiny flats in high-rise buildings. Many buildings were not very stable, and sometimes fell down with the people still inside. The flats had no kitchens or gardens, so people had to buy hot food from take-aways, and string washing between the buildings. They threw their rubbish into the streets, making the city dirty and smelly. Water had to be collected from a public water trough. Only rich people had piped water in their homes.

Did rich Romans have feasts?

Rich Romans really enjoyed having friends round for a feast. They served dozens of tasty dishes such as oysters, stuffed dormice, roast peacock and boiled ostrich. The Romans did not sit on chairs to eat, instead they lounged on couches. They ate with their fingers or with a spoon. Some rich Romans were so greedy they tried every dish and, in order to make room for more, they made themselves sick. They even had a special room for people to be sick in. It was called the vomitorium!

Who fought for sport?

The Romans loved to go to the amphitheatre to watch violent shows, which they called 'games'. At the amphitheatre, gladiators fought each other, often to the death. Some gladiators had to fight wild animals, such as lions, with spears, flaming torches or even their bare hands.

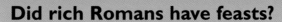

Quick-fire Quiz

1. When did Rome become a republic?
a) 509 BC
b) 409 BC
c) 309 BC

2. Who ruled the republic?
a) The emperor
b) The Senate
c) The king

3. What was a gladiator?
a) A public bath
b) A country house
c) A fighter

4. Who brought up Romulus and Remus?
a) Rich ladies
b) A wolf
c) The consuls

Gladiator

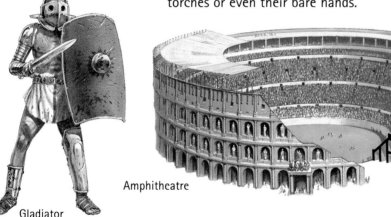

Amphitheatre

Where did Romans relax?

Most Romans went to the public baths to relax. These were more like leisure centres than places to wash. You could play games, read, chat to friends, work out in the gym or take a stroll in the gardens. You could even get your hair cut or have a massage.

113

The Roman Empire

The Roman republic ended in 27 BC, when Emperor Augustus set up a Roman empire. However, in AD 395 the empire was split into two. The western part (based in Rome) fell to tribes the Romans called 'barbarians' in AD 476. The eastern part, ruled from Constantinople (now Istanbul) lasted until AD 1453.

Did the Romans build bridges?

The Romans were very clever builders and engineers. They built huge stone bridges called viaducts to carry roads, and aqueducts (stone channels to carry water) across valleys. They also built many fine cities, linking them with long, straight roads.

What did the Romans trade?

Roman trade routes spread throughout Europe and into China and India. Their ships took many goods such as wine, olive oil and farm products as well as works of art to distant ports. They brought back exotic goods such as wild animals, ivory and silk.

Roman ship

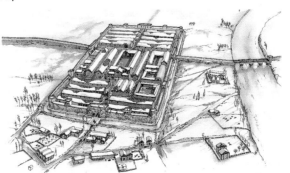

Which Roman leader was murdered?

Julius Caesar was a great general who made himself dictator (sole ruler) for life. Although he brought peace and passed good laws, the Senate thought he was too powerful. So on March 15, 44 BC, a group of them stabbed him to death.

Julius Caesar

Where did Roman soldiers live?

Soldiers on the move lived in leather tents. At other times, they lived in large forts with workshops, stables and hospitals. The men shared simple rooms, but the officers had houses.

How did Romans protect their cities?

In later times, the Romans needed to protect their cities from attack by the barbarian tribes that swept across Europe. They built thick walls around their towns and forts which could be defended easily by armed soldiers.

What did Roman soldiers wear?

Roman soldiers wore armour of metal strips joined together with straps, over a woollen tunic. They carried a shield to protect the lower body. On the move, they carried everything on their backs – weapons, tools and a kit bag.

Why was Rome so successful?

A well-organized, full-time army was the key to Rome's success. Highly trained soldiers were split into legions of 6,000 men made up of ten cohorts, and then into centuries of 100 men, under the command of a centurion (officer).

Who met in the catacombs?

Early Christians were persecuted by the Romans who thought they were plotting against the emperor. The Christians met in secret in the catacombs (underground burial chambers) beneath Rome. Many Christians were put to death in the arena to entertain the crowds. Some were made to fight unarmed against gladiators or lions. Emperor Constantine was converted to Christianity in AD 313, and about 60 years later it became the empire's official religion.

How were soldiers like a tortoise?

When they attacked an enemy fort, Roman soldiers protected themselves by forming a 'testudo' (tortoise). They held their shields over their heads so that they overlapped.

Who attacked Rome with elephants?

In 218 BC, Hannibal, a military leader from Carthage in North Africa, led 10,000 soldiers and 38 elephants through Spain and across the Alps to attack Rome. Hannibal won three important victories but only 12 elephants survived.

115

The Mayan Empire

The Maya Indians built a vast empire that covered parts of Mexico, Guatemala and Honduras in the jungles of Central America. It reached its peak from AD 300–800 but, over the next 200 years, it collapsed and was taken over by the Toltecs.

What clothes did Mayans wear?

Mayan men wore simple loin cloths. If it was cold they also wore a cloak called a 'manta'. Men dressed up in elaborate headdresses decorated with quetzal or macaw feathers. The more important the person, the bigger his hat! Women wore simple smock-like dresses.

God-king   Noble   Warrior   Priest

Who ruled the Maya?

Every Mayan city-state had its own royal family. They were ruled by a warrior god-king who led his people into battle. Next in importance were nobles, warriors and priests. Then came craftsmen and merchants, and last were peasants and labourers. The Maya worshipped the jaguar and noble Mayan warriors wore jaguar skins and headdresses. They thought that this would help to make them as fierce and brave in battle as a jaguar.

What were Mayan cities like?

The Maya were the first people in America to build big cities. These cities, which lay deep in the jungle, were full of grand pyramids, temples and palaces built of local limestone. The walls were covered with plaster and sometimes painted red. This colour was especially important to the Maya, for religious reasons. Walls were sometimes decorated with paintings of gods and hieroglyphs.

Did the Maya build pyramids?

The Maya built huge, stone-stepped pyramids with temples and an observatory at the top. The Castillo, the main pyramid in the Mayan city of Chichen Itza, has four stairways, each with 91 steps. These, together with the step at the temple entrance, add up to 365 – the number of days in a year.

Did Mayans study the stars?

The Maya were expert astronomers and studied the moon, stars and planets. They were also skilled mathematicians, and had a complicated calendar for counting the days and years. They used their knowledge to predict special events such as an eclipse.

Could Mayans read and write?

The Maya wrote in hieroglyphs (picture writing). They carved important inscriptions on huge stone monuments called stelae. They also wrote detailed accounts of important events in books made of bark or on animal skins. When the Spanish conquered the area in the early 1500s, they burned most of these books.

Did the Maya play ball?

The Maya played a religious ball game called Pok-a-tok. The players, who were bandaged to prevent injury, bounced a solid rubber ball to each other using their elbows, hips and thighs. The game was won by the first team to hit the ball through a stone ring mounted on the wall.

What gods did they worship?

The Mayans had over 150 gods. The most important was the sun god, who went down into the Underworld at sunset and became the jaguar god. They sometimes sacrificed captured enemies to their gods.

Timeline

Key dates in the development of ancient civilizations are recorded here – from the first cave paintings, through the creation and establishment of great empires to the sacking of Rome by the Vandals.

25,000 BC to 2000 BC

c.25,000 BC Stone Age people painted cave walls
c.10,000–9000 BC Start of agriculture in Near East
8000–7000 BC First permanent houses built; walled cities developed in Near East and Turkey
6000–5000 BC Looms used for weaving in Near East
5000 BC People began farming in Nile Valley in Egypt
4000–3000 BC Sumerian civilization in Mesopotamia; invented cuneiform writing; used ploughs and wheel
3372 BC First date in Mayan calendar
3000 BC Lower and Upper Egypt united under a single pharaoh
3000 BC Troy flourished as a city-state in Anatolia
c.2800 BC Stonehenge built in England
2800–2400 BC City-states of Sumer at their most powerful
2500 BC Rise of Indus Valley people
2700–2200 BC Old Kingdom in Egypt; first step pyramids built
2690 BC Huang Ti (Yellow emperor) ruled in China; according to legend, silk was discovered by his wife Hsi-Ling Shi
2600 BC Sphinx and Great Pyramids built in Egypt
2500 BC First European civilization, the Minoans, grew up on Greek island of Crete
2360 BC Arabians migrated to Mesopotamia and set up Babylonian and Assyrian kingdoms

2250 BC Hsai dynasty in power in China
2050 BC Start of Middle Kingdom of Egypt
2000 BC Hittites arrived in Anatolia (now Turkey)
2000 BC Mycenaeans invaded Greece

1999 BC to 1000 BC

1925 BC Hittites conquered Babylon
1830 BC First dynasty of Babylonian empire founded
1814–1782 BC Assyria extended empire
1792–1750 BC Hammurabi the Great ruled Babylon; empire declined after his death
1760 BC Shang dynasty founded in China
1750–1500 BC Hittites spread throughout area; invaded Syria
1650–1450 BC Mycenaean power centred on Mycenae and Pylos
1550–1050 BC New Kingdom in Egypt; Valley of Kings used for pharaohs' tombs
1500–1166 BC Egypt at peak of power
1500 BC Aryans invaded Indus Valley
c1500 BC Mayans farm land in Central America; developed a calendar and writing
1450 BC Minoan civilization collapsed and Mycenaeans took over
1350–1250 BC Assyrian empire extends
1200 BC Trojan Wars: Mycenaeans invaded and destroyed Troy in Anatolia
1200 BC Hittites' empire collapsed after invasion of Phoenicians; Phoenicians became the world's most powerful sea traders
1150 BC Israelites arrived in Canaan
1100 BC Mycenaean civilization collapsed
c.1122 BC Zhou dynasty in China came to power after defeating armies of Shang dynasty
1050 BC Phoenicians developed alphabet (basis for all modern alphabets)
c.1000 BC Dorians invaded Greece; start of Dark Ages
c.1000 BC Kingdom of Kush in Africa began
1000 BC Israel ruled by King David

999 BC to 500 BC

900–625 BC Assyria and Babylon at war

900–700 BC Etruscans flourished in upper Italy

c.814 BC Carthage founded

800 BC Greek poet Homer wrote about Trojan Wars and Greek legends

800 BC Olmecs in Mexico built temples

753 BC Traditional date for founding of Rome

750–600 BC Celts appeared in Central Europe and spread throughout western Europe

c.750–682 BC Kingdom of Kush defeated Egypt; Nubians rule over Egypt

729 BC Assyrians ruled Babylon

700 BC Assyrians took over Phoenicia and Israel

700–500 BC Rise of Athens and other Greek city-states

689 BC Assyrians destroyed Babylon

671–664 BC Assyrians ruled Egypt

668–627 BC Assurbanipal increased power of Assyria

609 BC Assyrian empire ended

605–562 BC Nebuchadnezzar rebuilt Babylon

c.600 BC Zoroaster reforms the ancient Persian religion

590 BC Babylonians took over Jerusalem

c.550 BC Persian empire became powerful

551 BC Confucius was born in China

539 BC Persians took over Babylon and Phoenicia

525–404 BC Persians ruled Egypt

509 BC Roman kings replaced by Roman republic

508 BC Athens became a democracy

500 BC Italian Etruscan empire very powerful

499 BC to AD 1

490–480 BC Persian wars between Greeks and Persians; Greeks defeated Persians in 479 BC

c.477–405 BC Golden Age of Athens

463–221 BC Time of warring states in China

450–400 BC Etruscan empire declined

431–404 BC Peloponnesian wars between Athens and Sparta; Sparta won in 404 BC

390 BC Celts attacked Rome

338 BC Philip of Macedonia conquered Greece

336 BC Alexander the Great became king of Macedonia and Greece

333–323 BC Alexander the Great conquered Phoenicia, Egypt, Persia and parts of India

321–184 BC Mauryan empire founded in India

300 BC Mayans started to build stone cities

275 BC Romans took over all Italy

265 BC Romans started to conquer Europe

264–146 BC Carthage at war with Rome (Punic Wars)

250 BC Celtic tribes at peak of power

221 BC Emperor Qin united China in first dynasty

206 BC– AD 220 Han dynasty in China

218 BC Hannibal invaded Rome on elephants

202 BC Hannibal defeated by Romans

146 BC Carthage defeated; North Africa became part of Roman empire

55 BC Julius Caesar invaded Britain but had to retreat

52 BC Caesar conquered Celtic Gaul (France)

45 BC Caesar became dictator of Rome

44 BC Caesar assassinated

30 BC Egypt taken over by the Romans

27 BC Octavian becomes first Roman emperor, Augustus

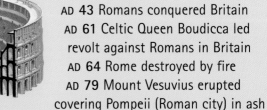

AD 1 to AD 800

AD 43 Romans conquered Britain

AD 61 Celtic Queen Boudicca led revolt against Romans in Britain

AD 64 Rome destroyed by fire

AD 79 Mount Vesuvius erupted covering Pompeii (Roman city) in ash

c.AD 150 Roman empire most powerful

AD 250 European barbarian tribes attacked Rome

AD 284 Roman empire split into east and west

AD 268 Goths sacked Athens and Sparta

AD 330 Constantinople (now Istanbul) became capital of eastern Roman empire

AD 300-700 Mayan civilization at height

AD 406 Tribe called Vandals overran Gaul

AD 410 Rome sacked by Visigoths; Romans left Britain

AD 455 Rome sacked by Vandals

AD 476 Last western Roman emperor deposed; eastern empire continued until AD 1453 as Byzantine empire

AD 800 Mayan cities abandoned; civilization collapsed; Toltecs took over

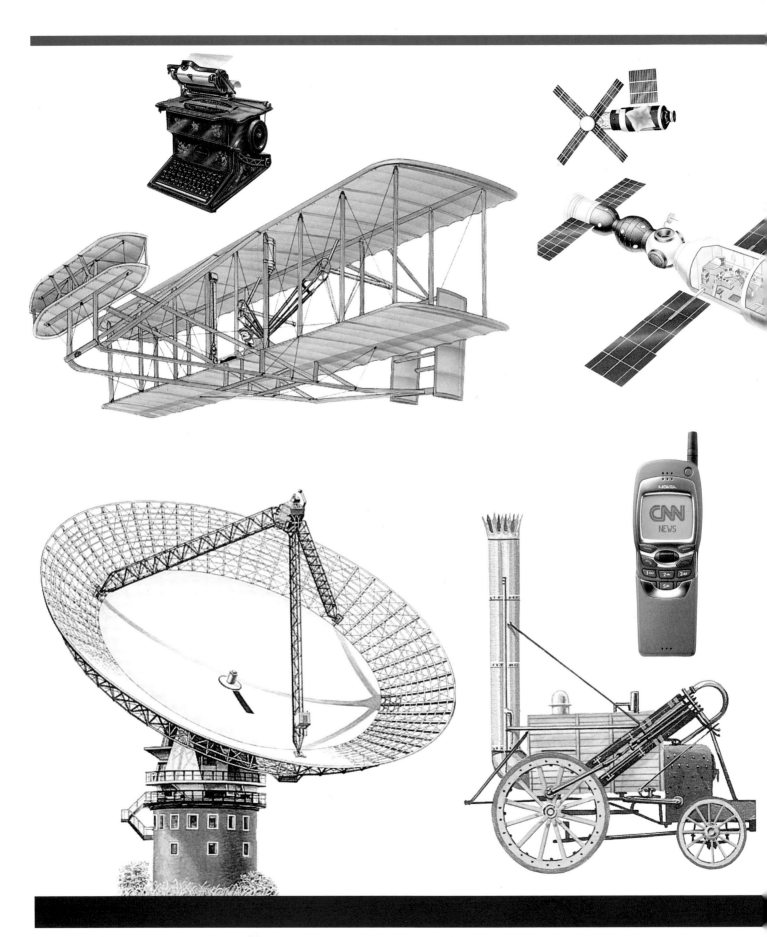

INVENTIONS

Writing and Printing

The first true writing system was invented by the Sumerians over 5,000 years ago. They used pictures called pictograms to stand for objects, ideas and sounds. Today, the written or printed word is central to human communication.

Who invented printing?

Block printing was invented by the Chinese nearly 2,000 years ago. They carved characters on wooden blocks, covered them in ink and stamped them on to paper. Modern printing, with movable metal type, began in the 1440s when a German, Johannes Gutenberg, developed the printing press.

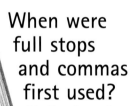

When were full stops and commas first used?

Medieval monks and scribes produced handwritten, beautifully decorated illuminated manuscripts. To make the manuscripts easier to read, the scribes separated words with spaces, used capital and small letters and introduced a system of punctuation, including full stops and commas.

Why did typewriters make you crazy?

People are often scared of a new inventions. When the first typewriter went on sale in 1874, some doctors said that using one could make you go mad! However, the typewriter was a huge success for its American inventor, Christopher Latham Sholes. The first successful portable typewriter appeared in the early 1900s and electric typewriters whizzed into action in 1901.

Who invented the paper clip?

The paper clip is such a simple and useful design, it is surprising that it is quite a recent invention. It first appeared in 1900, invented by Johan Vaalar, a young scientist who worked for an invention office in Norway. Before the paper clip, people used straight pins or ribbons tied through holes in the corner of the pages to fasten papers together temporarily.

Who was Mr Biro?

Ladislao Biro, a Hungarian journalist, invented the ballpoint pen in 1938. It contained a tube of quick-drying ink which rolled evenly on to the paper thanks to a tiny movable ball at the tip.

What was the first advertisement?

The oldest known piece of publicity is an ancient Egyptian papyrus dating from almost 5,000 years ago. The message is written in hieroglyphs, or picture writing, and offers a reward for finding a runaway slave.

Is there really lead in a pencil?

No! The 'lead' in a pencil is not made from the metal lead at all. It's made from graphite mixed with clay. The modern pencil was invented independently by Frenchman Nicholas-Jacque Conte and Austrian Josef Hardtmuth in 1795. Their invention was a great success – it could be easily sharpened and erased.

Quick-fire Quiz

1. Which civilization wrote in hieroglyphs?
a) Ancient Egypt
b) Ancient Greece
c) Ancient Rome

2. Where was the printing press invented?
a) Britain
b) China
c) Germany

3. When was the pencil invented?
a) 1595
b) 1695
c) 1795

4. What did Ladislao Biro invent?
a) Felt-tip pens
b) Ballpoint pens
c) Fountain pens

How does a mouse draw?

A computer mouse allows you to direct the cursor around the screen to give the computer commands. Using a mouse, designers can draw new details on to a picture. The computer mouse was invented in the United States in 1964 by Douglas Englehart. He also invented a foot-controlled 'rat' but it never caught on.

Why were felt-tip pens invented?

The Japanese inventor hoped that the pen's soft tip would make people's handwriting more graceful – like the brushstrokes in Japanese writing. The first felt-tips went on sale in Japan in 1962.

Medicine

Doctors in the ancient world used herbs, surgery and 'magic' to treat illnesses. Scientific medicine began in the 1600s with the invention of the microscope and an understanding of anatomy. Technical advances in the 1900s led to modern medicine.

Who were the first doctors?

The earliest doctors were physicians in ancient Egypt and China. In Egypt, physicians used drugs and potions. Surgeons treated injuries, and priests dealt with evil spirits. The first known physician was an Egyptian, Imhotep, who lived about 4,600 years ago.

When were bacteria discovered?

The Dutch instrument-maker Antonie van Leeuwenhoek made the first high-powered microscope. It could magnify up to 200 times. In 1683, he published drawings of bacteria – tiny living things that can cause disease. He was building on the work of English scientist Robert Hooke who, 20 years before, had discovered that living things were made up of small cells.

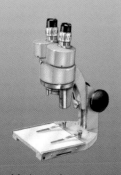

Modern microscope

Who discovered how blood flows?

In 1628, an English doctor, William Harvey, found that the heart pumps blood into the arteries. He showed that it circulates all around the body and returns to the heart along the veins.

Are drugs made from plants?

Most modern drugs are made from chemicals, but many were originally made from plants. For example, the heart drug, digitalis, comes from foxgloves. Quinine from the cinchona tree is used to treat malaria and aspirin is made from the bark of the willow.

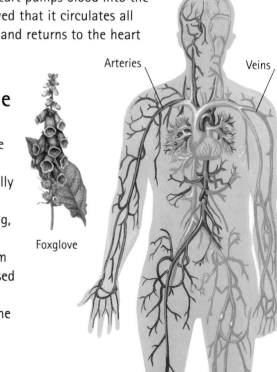

Arteries

Veins

Foxglove

Can artificial limbs move?

Artificial arm and hand

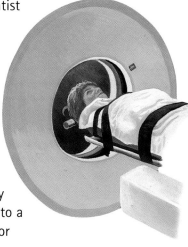

Prosthetic hook

Back in the Middle Ages, the French surgeon Amboise Paré used springs and cogs to move artificial arms and legs. Today, whole legs and arms can be replaced with computer-controlled plastic or metal limbs. In some cases, nerve-endings in the patient's limb send messages to motors in the artificial limb to make it move.

How can we 'see' our bones?

We can see the bones in our bodies by taking X-rays of them. In 1895, the German scientist Wilhelm Röntgen first discovered that X-rays could pass through paper, wood and flesh, but not through metal or bone. Within months, doctors were using X-rays to photograph bones in the body.

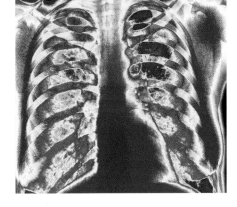

What is a body scan?

In 1972, British scientist Godfrey Hounsfield developed a Computerized Tomography (CT) scanner to take pictures of the inside of the body. CT scanners take thousands of X-rays of the brain and body and build them up into a kind of 3-D picture for doctors to study.

Who made surgery safer?

In 1865, the Scottish surgeon Joseph Lister was the first doctor to use antiseptics during surgery to stop patients dying from infections. He sprayed carbolic acid round the operating theatre and soaked dressings in it to kill germs.

Early carbolic acid spray

Quick-fire Quiz

1. What is digitalis made from?
a) Willows
b) Cinchona
c) Foxgloves

2. When were drawings of bacteria first published?
a) 1583
b) 1683
c) 1783

3. What did Harvey discover?
a) Blood circulation
b) X-rays
c) Bacteria

4. Who first used antiseptics?
a) Watson and Crick
b) Godfrey Hounsfield
c) Joseph Lister

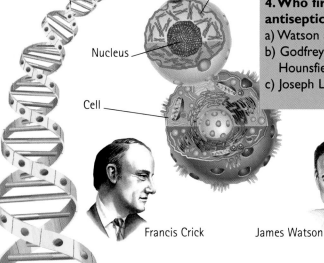

Chromosomes
DNA
Nucleus
Cell
Francis Crick
James Watson

What is the double helix?

DNA (deoxyribonucleic acid) is the chemical that controls how cells behave and reproduce. In 1953, two scientists Francis Crick from England and the American James Watson worked out that DNA was made up of a twisted spiral — a double helix.

Buildings

The first permanent buildings were put up about 10,000 years ago. At first people used natural materials, such as wood and stone, and most of the work was done by hand with simple tools. Today, hi-tech machines and the latest materials are used to build huge skyscrapers.

What is a Gothic building?

The Gothic style of building began in the mid-1100s in western Europe. It was mainly used for churches and cathedrals, which often had tall spires and towers, pointed arches, carved stonework and fancy windows. The workers had to scramble up and down wooden scaffolding tied up with rope, as there were no cranes to help them.

What was Stonehenge for?

Stonehenge, England, was built about 5,000 years ago. The standing megaliths (big stones) were arranged to mark the midsummer sunrise and the midwinter moonrise. It may have been a religious meeting place or a huge outdoor calendar used to study the movement of the Sun.

Can bridges carry water?

Bridges for carrying water were first built by the Assyrians, around 700 BC. Three hundred years later, the Romans improved the technique and built huge stone aqueducts to supply their cities with running water. Many Roman aqueducts still stand today.

Who designed a sail-like roof?

One of the most stunning modern buildings is the Opera House in Sydney Harbour, Australia. The architect, Jorn Utzon from Denmark, designed it to look like wind-filled sails. The main roof was made from concrete segments covered with thousands of ceramic tiles. The Opera House took 15 years to build. It was finished in 1973.

How old are the pyramids?

The first true pyramid was built in Egypt in about 2575 BC. Each of these huge tombs for the dead pharaohs took about 20 years to build. Thousands of workers dragged the huge stones up ramps and levered them into place with wooden poles.

Are there wire bridges?

In 1883, the Brooklyn Bridge in New York, United States, was the first suspension bridge built using steel cables, which can carry huge loads. Its designer, John Roebling, used over 1,900 kilometres of wire anchored with around 90,000 tonnes of masonry.

How are suspension bridges built?

The towers are built first. Steel ropes are suspended from the towers. Special machines spin these into strong steel cables. Next, long steel cables called hangers are attached to the suspending cables. Sections of the deck are lifted into place and fixed to the hangers.

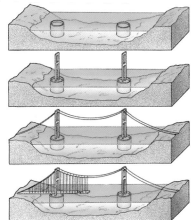
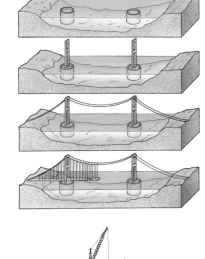

Do buildings have skeletons?

In the 1880s, architects had the idea of using a skeleton of steel and concrete columns to support the roof, walls and floors of tall buildings. They fixed the outer walls to this framework. The first skyscraper, built in Chicago in the United States, was ten storeys tall. Today many tower over 400 metres high.

127

Food and Agriculture

Farming probably began about 10,000 years ago in the Middle East. Early farmers harvested wild wheat and barley and sowed some of the seeds to grow new crops. Gradually, farmers developed tools and, after the 1700s, farms began to be mechanised.

Did early farmers use ploughs?

Wooden ploughs developed from digging sticks used in Mesopotamia over 5,500 years ago. At first, people pulled ploughs, but then oxen were used. Ploughs with iron blades to break up heavy soil were made about 4,000 years later. More land could be cultivated with these, so farms grew larger.

Who invented the milking machine?

In 1860, American Lee Colvin had an idea to speed up milking. Hoses linked rubber caps on the cow's teats to a bucket and bellows. Pumping the bellows milked the cow. Modern milking machines use a similar idea. Today, many milking parlours are computer-controlled.

Cups fit over a cow's teats

Who first used windmills?

Windmills were first used in Persia over 1,200 years ago. By the 1200s they were being used in Europe, mainly to grind grain. During the 1700s and 1800s thousands were built to grind grain, power saws, raise materials from mines and pump water.

What is organic farming?

Artificial fertilizers were first made commercially by Sir John Bennet Lawes in England in 1842. Now many farmers use them to increase crop yields. In the 1970s, some farmers, worried about the effects of these fertilizers, returned to organic farming, in which only natural fertilizers are used.

What is a combine harvester?

A combine harvester reaps, threshes, loads grain on to trailers and bales the leftover straw. The first one, built by an American, Hyram Moore, in the late 1830s, was pulled by horses. Later, tractors were used. By the 1930s, they were diesel-powered.

Why are crops sprayed?

Crops are sprayed with pesticides to kill unwanted pests that could destroy the crop. The first synthetic insecticide, DDT, was isolated in 1874 by the German, Othmar Zeidler. It was first made commercially in 1939, when a German chemist, Paul Muller, found it could kill insects, including the mosquitoes that carry disease.

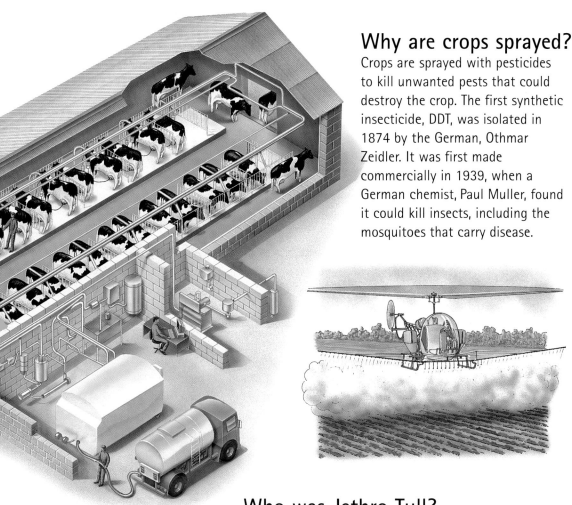

Quick-fire Quiz

1. Who first used windmills?
a) The Chinese
b) The Persians
c) The Sumerians

2. When was the seed drill invented?
a) 1501
b) 1601
c) 1701

3. Who invented the milking machine?
a) Lee Colvin
b) Jethro Tull
c) Hyram Moore

4. What is DDT?
a) A fertilizer
b) An insecticide
c) A machine

Who was Jethro Tull?

Seed used to be scattered on the fields by hand. Then, in 1701, English farmer Jethro Tull developed a machine that could drill and sow seeds in straight lines. His machine fed seeds at an even rate into a furrow made by a coulter, or blade.

Can farm animals be cloned?

Scientists can make clones (identical copies) of living things by growing a new organism from a cell taken from the 'parent'. In February 1997, Dolly the sheep made history – she was a clone of her mother. She was grown from one of her mother's cells instead of from an egg. A year later, a cow was produced in the same way.

129

At Home

The first homes were caves and simple huts. Slowly, people developed new skills to build better homes, preserve food and make their lives more comfortable. Modern homes have electricity, gas, water and drainage and lots of household goods and furniture.

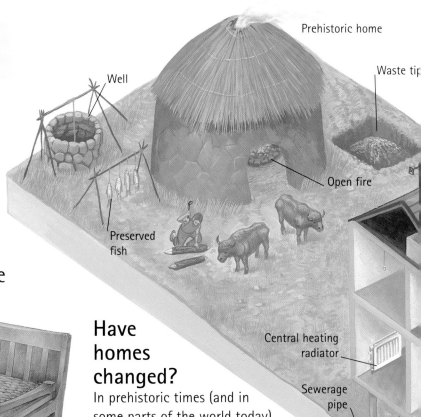

Prehistoric home

Well

Waste tip

Open fire

Preserved fish

Central heating radiator

Sewerage pipe

Water pipe

Who invented furniture?

Simple wooden furniture has probably been around since people began to build permanent homes. In Egypt, beautiful carved furniture was being made over 3,500 years ago. These luxurious articles were found in a tomb for a dead pharaoh to use in the afterlife.

Have homes changed?

In prehistoric times (and in some parts of the world today) people lived in homes built from mud or stones, cooked on open fires and got water from wells. Modern homes are stronger and more comfortable. From the 1880s homes were wired with electricity, giving light and power at the flick of a switch.

When did irons 'go electric'?

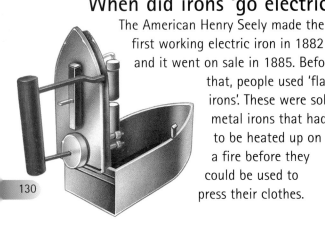

The American Henry Seely made the first working electric iron in 1882 and it went on sale in 1885. Before that, people used 'flat irons'. These were solid metal irons that had to be heated up on a fire before they could be used to press their clothes.

How was food kept cool?

Over 4,000 years ago, people stored food in ice pits to keep it cool. Early domestic refrigerators – insulated cabinets for holding ice – first appeared in the United States around 1850. The first mechanical one, powered by a steam pump, was the bright idea of German engineer Karl von Linde in 1879. Within 12 years he had sold 12,000 in Germany and the United States. The first electrical refrigerator, developed by Swedish engineers von Platen and Munters, went on sale in 1925.

How old is the flushing toilet?

Over 5,000 years ago, the Mesopotamians had special seats with holes and water running underneath to take away the waste. This idea was developed further by the English inventor John Harington, who published the earliest design for a flushing toilet with a cistern in 1596. The first practical flushing toilet was made by Alexander Cumming in the 1770s.

Modern home

Television satellite dish

Electrical power

Flushing toilet

Chamber pot

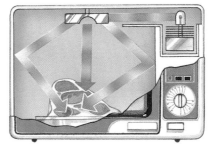

Which waves can melt chocolate?

American Percy Spencer discovered microwave cooking by accident. He'd been working on ways of using invisible microwaves to detect aircraft. When he found that these waves had melted a chocolate bar in his pocket, he realised they could be used to cook food too. In 1946, the first microwave oven was developed and in 1955, commercial ones appeared.

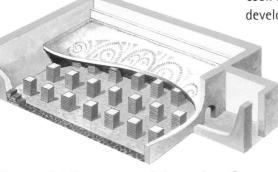

How old is central heating?

The ancient Romans first developed a method of heating their houses with hot air nearly 2,000 years ago. Called a hypocaust, warm air, heated by burning fuel in a furnace, flowed through tiled flues in the walls into the spaces beneath the floor, heating the rooms above.

Who lit up homes?

In 1878, the Briton Joseph Swan demonstrated his electric light bulb. A year later, the American inventor Thomas Edison made a long-lasting light bulb with a carbon filament, which went on sale in 1880. The two men eventually set up a joint company to make light bulbs.

Clothes and Fabrics

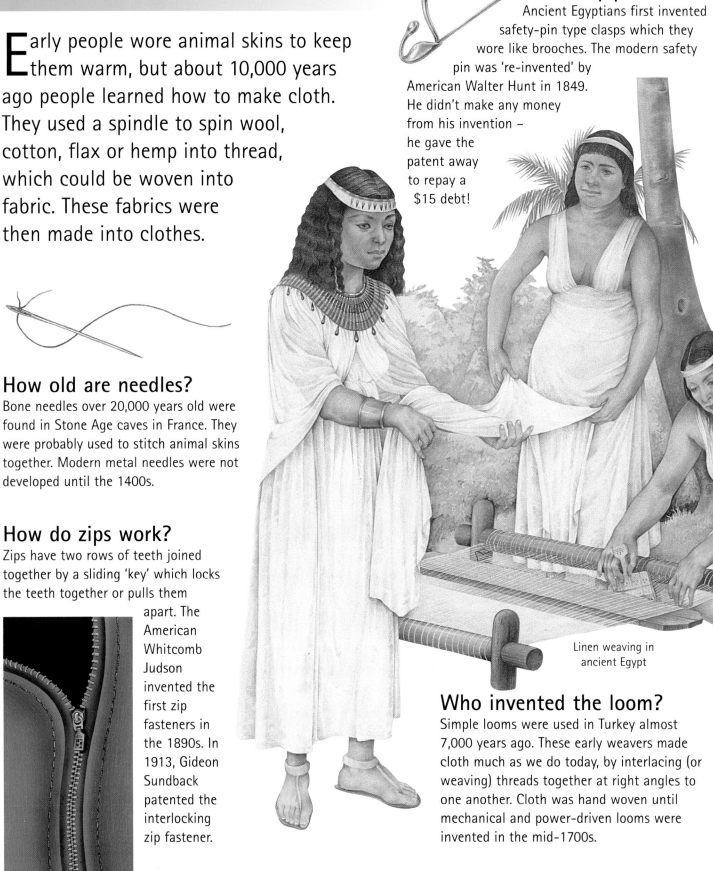

Early people wore animal skins to keep them warm, but about 10,000 years ago people learned how to make cloth. They used a spindle to spin wool, cotton, flax or hemp into thread, which could be woven into fabric. These fabrics were then made into clothes.

How old are needles?

Bone needles over 20,000 years old were found in Stone Age caves in France. They were probably used to stitch animal skins together. Modern metal needles were not developed until the 1400s.

How do zips work?

Zips have two rows of teeth joined together by a sliding 'key' which locks the teeth together or pulls them apart. The American Whitcomb Judson invented the first zip fasteners in the 1890s. In 1913, Gideon Sundback patented the interlocking zip fastener.

Who wore safety pins?

Ancient Egyptians first invented safety-pin type clasps which they wore like brooches. The modern safety pin was 're-invented' by American Walter Hunt in 1849. He didn't make any money from his invention – he gave the patent away to repay a $15 debt!

Linen weaving in ancient Egypt

Who invented the loom?

Simple looms were used in Turkey almost 7,000 years ago. These early weavers made cloth much as we do today, by interlacing (or weaving) threads together at right angles to one another. Cloth was hand woven until mechanical and power-driven looms were invented in the mid-1700s.

Are shoes made in factories?

Shoes have been around for thousands of years and, until the mid-1800s, they were all handmade. These Native American moccasins were made by hand from soft deer-skin and adorned with coloured porcupine quills. This took many hours. Today a pair of shoes can be made in minutes by a machine in a factory.

Who tanned leather?

Leather clothing, footwear and household goods were used over 5,000 years ago in Mesopotamia. In the past, people 'tanned' leather by rubbing the hides with the juices of bark and roots that contain the chemical tannin. (This is where 'tanning' gets its name.) Sometimes skins were soaked in salt and the chemical alum to preserve them.

Quick-fire Quiz

1. When were zips invented?
a) 1690s
b) 1790s
c) 1890s

2. Who first made silk?
a) Romans
b) Native Americans
c) Chinese

3. Who invented the spinning jenny?
a) Whitcomb Judson
b) Elias Howe
c) James Hargreaves

4. What did George de Mestral make?
a) Velcro
b) Lock-stitch sewing machine
c) Safety pin

Which machine was destroyed?

French tailor Barthélemy Thimonnier developed a sewing machine in 1829. Other tailors destroyed it, fearing it would put them out of work. In the United States, a lock-stitch machine was invented by Walter Hunt in 1833 and Elias Howe made a better machine in 1845. Sewing machines became widely available in the late 1850s.

Early sewing machine

What was a spinning jenny?

In 1764, Englishman James Hargreaves invented an automatic spinning machine, the spinning jenny. It could spin eight reels of thread at once, compared with the one reel made by an ordinary spinning wheel.

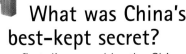

What was China's best-kept secret?

Silk was first discovered by the Chinese over 4,600 years ago. They set up farms to breed silk worms about 3,500 years ago but kept the method a secret for another 2,000 years. Silk was so valuable that the Chinese traded it for gold and silver.

What is Velcro?

Swiss engineer George de Mestral spent eight years developing Velcro. It is made from two nylon strips, one covered with tiny loops, the other with tiny hooks. The strips stick to each other when pressed together but can easily be ripped apart. Velcro went on sale in the mid-1960s.

133

Useful Materials

Once, people used natural materials such as wood or cotton to make things. Later, they discovered how to extract metals from ore found in the ground. Today, synthetic materials, such as nylon, plastic and fibreglass, are used to make many goods from cars to clothes.

Pottery-making in ancient China

Is glass made from sand?

Glass is made by heating silica (sand), limestone and soda to very high temperatures. It can then be coloured and shaped. Many medieval churches have windows made of stained glass, like this one. The oldest surviving window, in Augsberg Cathedral, Germany, dates from 1065.

Why do cars rust?

Iron and steel objects rust in damp air because the iron changes into a red-brown iron oxide, a mixture of iron and oxygen. In 1913, the Briton Harry Brearley added the metal chromium to steel to make the first successful rust-resistant stainless steel.

What is steel?

Steel, a strong metal made from iron, was first developed over 3,000 years ago. In 1856, the British inventor Henry Bessemer devised a cheap way of producing steel. Molten iron was poured into a converter and hot air or oxygen was blown over it. Most of the carbon in the iron was burned, turning it into steel.

Steel-making

Where was china made?

Pottery goods have been made for about 9,000 years, but fine china, or porcelain, was only invented about 1,200 years ago in China. The art remained a secret until just over 300 years ago, when fine porcelain goods were taken to the West.

Who first used plants to make materials?

People have made useful materials from plant fibres for thousands of years and many are still used today. About 5,000 years ago, cotton plants were first cultivated in India and the Chinese used the fibrous stems of hemp to make rope. The ancient Egyptians made fine linen fabric from flax stems.

Quick-fire Quiz

1. What was made from hemp?
a) China
b) Rope
c) Plastic

2. When was polythene discovered?
a) 1733
b) 1833
c) 1933

3. Where was rubber discovered?
a) China
b) Brazil
c) India

4. Who made steel cheap?
a) Bessemer
b) Brearley
c) Carothers

Are plastics oily?

All plastics, such as polyvinylchloride (PVC), polythene, nylon and some paints, are made from chemicals found in oil, natural gas or coal. Polythene was first discovered by accident in 1933 by chemists working at ICI in Britain. Two years later, nylon was made by Wallace Carothers in the United States.

Is fibreglass strong?

Fibreglass material is made by mixing glass fibres and plastic. It was developed in the United States in the 1930s. It is flame-resistant, does not rust and is tough enough to make car bodies or boats. It is also used to insulate buildings.

Fibreglass canoe

Bakelite radio

What was Bakelite?

In 1909, a Belgian-American chemist named Leo Hendrik Baekeland made the world's first artificial plastic – Bakelite. As it did not conduct heat or electricity it was ideal for making electrical goods.

Is rubber liquid?

Natural rubber is made from the thick, runny sap, or latex, of rubber trees. The latex is collected, strained, mixed with acid to solidify it and rolled into sheets. Wild rubber was discovered in Brazil in the early 1800s and was first used for waterproofing. Today we mostly use synthetic rubbers, developed about 60 years ago.

135

Toys and Games

Toys and games have been around for thousands of years. Some toys were just for fun, but many prepared children for adult life. Games also developed from the skills needed to hunt and fight. In some ancient cultures, sport was part of their religion.

How old is football?

No-one is sure when football began, but by the 1200s street football was a popular sport. There were no pitches, goals, or rules. The sole aim was to get the ball to your team's home ground. Men and boys chased the ball through the streets, knocking people out of their way. It got so rough that in 1314 King Edward II of England banned football in London.

When was chess invented?

Chess was invented about 1,400 years ago in India or China to help develop war skills. The board represents the field of battle and the pieces are different ranks and officers. The object of the game is to capture your opponent's king.

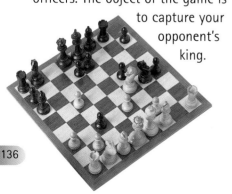

What's a home run?

In baseball, if the batter hits the ball and races round all four bases in one go, it's called a home run. Baseball developed in the United States in the 1800s from the British game of rounders. The first organized game was played in 1846.

When were jigsaws first made?

Jigsaws date back to the 1760s, when European map makers pasted maps on to wood and cut them up into pieces. These early wooden jigsaws did not interlock and were used for lessons rather than fun.

Who first played board games?

People first began to play board games around 4,000 years ago. This game from Mesopotamia dates from between 3000 and 2000 BC and is one of the oldest found. It has a marked board, dice and counters but no rules have survived, so no-one knows its name or how it was played.

Which captains lost their heads?

About 500 years ago, the Aztecs and Mayas of Central America played a ball game called tlochtli. The aim was to toss a rubber ball into the opposing team's end of the court, using only elbows, hips and knees. A team won outright if they hit the ball through a ring placed high up on the wall. The captain of the losing Aztec team was sometimes beheaded!

Quick-fire Quiz

1. **Where were the Olympics first held?**
a) Central America
b) Ancient Greece
c) Babylon

2. **How old is chess?**
a) 1,400 years old
b) 140 years old
c) 14,000 years old

3. **What game was banned in London?**
a) Baseball
b) Football
c) Cricket

4. **What did Ralph Baer invent?**
a) A card game
b) A board game
c) A home video game

What is a Game Boy™?

In 1989, Nintendo of Japan launched their first hand-held video game – the Game Boy™. Even though the first games were very simple, the Game Boy™ was a huge success, selling over 100 million in four years. The first home video game – a simulated game of table tennis – was invented by the American Ralph Baer in 1972.

When was the first Olympic Games?

The first Games was a religious festival held in ancient Greece over 2,000 years ago. These ancient Games, held every four years, first featured just one race, but in time, with more contests, they lasted for five days. The modern Olympics date from 1896, and today over 7,000 athletes from 120 nations take part.

Which toy was named after an American president?

Teddy bears are named after the American president Theodore Roosevelt, called Teddy for short. Toy bears were the bright idea of a sweetshop owner who read a story about Roosevelt refusing to shoot a bear cub. He decided to stop selling sweets and make toy bears he called 'teddies' instead.

Energy

People use energy for all sorts of activities from powering cars to lighting their homes. Most of the energy we use is made by burning fossil fuels such as coal, gas and oil. Renewable energy sources such as solar, water and wind power can be used to generate electricity.

Arkwright's Mill

Did water-power run factories?

Watermills have been used for over 2,000 years to grind corn. In 1771, Richard Arkwright turned a watermill into a cloth-making factory, using the water wheel to power his new spinning machines.

What is a wind farm?

Modern windmills are used to turn machines called turbines which generate, or make, electricity. These wind turbines are grouped together in wind farms. The first large wind generator was built by the American Palmer Putnam in 1940.

Who made engines steam?

An English blacksmith, Thomas Newcomen, built the first practical steam engine in 1712. The Scotsman James Watt came up with an improved design and in 1782 his double-action steam engine was used to power factory machinery.

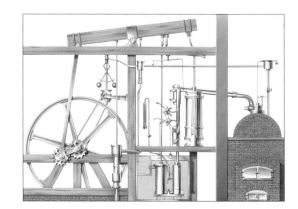

138

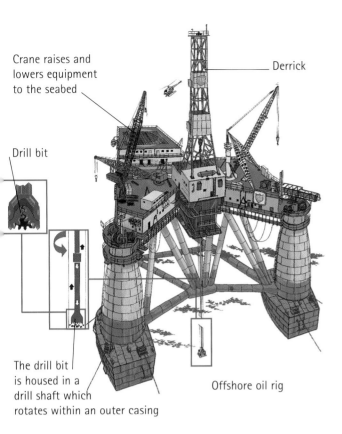

Crane raises and lowers equipment to the seabed

Derrick

Drill bit

The drill bit is housed in a drill shaft which rotates within an outer casing

Offshore oil rig

Can the Sun heat a home?
A few modern homes have solar panels in the roof. Some use the Sun's heat to warm water. Others contain electronic devices called photovoltaic (solar) cells to change sunlight into electricity. Solar power can run machines. The first practical solar-powered machine, a steam engine, was developed by Frenchman Augustin Mouchet in 1861.

Is oil found under the sea?
In the 1970s, large oil deposits were found under the North Sea. Oil wells were drilled 200 metres beneath the sea. Offshore oil rigs had to be built to pump the oil to the surface. These rigs are supported on steel or concrete structures that are sunk deep into the seabed.

Who split the atom?
In 1932, British scientists John Cockroft and Ernest Walton first split the atom, releasing huge amounts of energy. In the United States, in 1942, Italian-born Enrico Fermi and his team built the first successful nuclear reactor to control this energy. In 1954, the first nuclear power station was opened in Russia.

What is a hydrodam?
Hydroelectric power stations are often built inside dams called hydrodams. Water from a lake behind the dam gushes down pipes, turning turbines that drive generators and make electricity. The world's first major hydroelectric power station opened in 1895 at the Niagara Falls in North America.

What are fossil fuels?
Coal, oil and gas are called fossil fuels. Coal is the remains of ancient plants that lived and died in prehistoric forests. Oil and gas are made from the bodies of tiny dead sea creatures. The first coal-fired power station to generate electricity opened in 1882.

Calculations

When people first began to count, they could get by using just fingers and toes. But soon they invented tally sticks and number systems to record and calculate measurements. Numbers are the basis of all calculations. Today, most people use a modern version of numbers invented in Arabia (0 to 10).

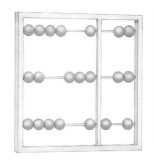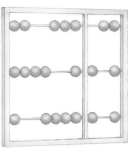

Who invented the abacus?

A simple abacus dates back to Mesopotamia, 5,000 years ago. The Chinese abacus, designed about 1,700 years ago, is made up of rows of beads representing units, tens, hundreds and thousands. It is a rapid tool for adding, subtracting, multiplying and dividing.

What was an astrolabe?

The astrolabe was originally a circular map of the heavens used by astronomers to measure the height of stars and planets. In the early Middle Ages, Arab scholars developed the astrolabe as an instrument to measure latitude and help them to navigate at sea.

Astrolabe

Moroccan students in the Middle Ages

What was the earliest money?

Long ago, people used to swap goods for the things they wanted. The people of ancient Lydia (now Turkey) were the first to make coins, about 2,700 years ago. They used electrum, a mixture of gold and silver. The Chinese invented paper bank notes about 1,200 years ago.

Who first used weights?

The first known standard weights and scales were used by the Babylonians about 4,600 years ago. The ancient Egyptians also used sensitive scales and weights to weigh precious stones and gold over 5,000 years ago.

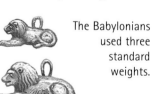

The Babylonians used three standard weights.

Who made the first mechanical calculator?

The first mechanical calculator was made by the Frenchman Blaise Pascal in 1642 when he was aged only 19. It had a row of toothed wheels with numbers around them. Numbers to be added or subtracted were dialled in and the answer appeared behind holes at the top. Modern electronic pocket calculators went on sale in 1971. They can do complicated calculations in seconds.

What was a handspan?

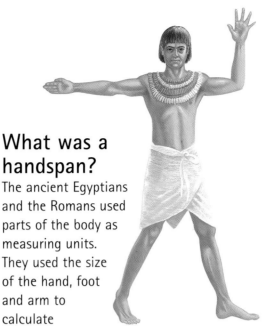

The ancient Egyptians and the Romans used parts of the body as measuring units. They used the size of the hand, foot and arm to calculate distances, but these measurements varied according to the size of the person making them. Eventually, standard measurements were adopted.

Quick-fire Quiz

1. What did a sundial measure?
a) Distance
b) Time
c) Weight

2. Where were coins invented?
a) Egypt
b) China
c) Turkey

3. What did Pascal build?
a) An abacus
b) A calculator
c) A clock

4. Fahrenheit made his mercury thermometer in?
a) 1614
b) 1714
c) 1814

What were the first clocks?

Sundials and shadow clocks, which use the Sun's passage across the sky to measure time, were first used in ancient Egypt to tell the time. The Babylonians divided the sundial's circle into 360 parts or degrees and divided it into 12 hours. In the Middle Ages, the hour- or sandglass was a popular 'clock'. Atomic clocks were first developed in 1969 and are accurate to one second in 1.6 million years!

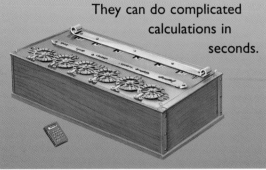

Sundial

Atomic clock

Sandglass

How do we measure temperature?

The first practical sealed alcohol thermometers, in which liquid rose up a tube as it heated, were made around 1660. In 1714, the German Gabriel Fahrenheit made a more accurate thermometer using mercury.

Alcohol thermometer

Who was Einstein?

Albert Einstein was a very clever German scientist who studied many things including energy and time. In 1915 he developed the theory of relativity, which says that time would slow down, length would shorten and mass would increase if you could travel almost as fast as the speed of light.

$E = mc^2$

141

Computers

Modern computers – electronic machines that can store and process masses of information – were first designed in the 1940s. Computers can do billions of calculations a second and we use them to carry out many tasks, from predicting the weather to making other machines.

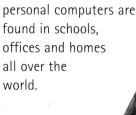

What are microchips?

In the 1960s, scientists came up with a new way to run computers. They used a tiny slice, or chip, of a material called silicon to make the electronic 'brain' that controls a computer. Today a tiny microchip contains up to 250,000 parts that tell it how to work. A computer uses different microchips to do different jobs.

Why were computers as big as a room?

The Americans John Mauchly and J. Prosper Eckert Jr built the first proper automatic computer (ENIAC) in 1945. It filled two whole rooms and weighed as much as five elephants. It was this large because it used 19,000 valves, each as big as a hand, to control the switches that made it work. Computers got smaller in the 1950s when tiny transistors replaced valves.

Who developed PCs?

The first successful personal computer, or PC, was developed by Steve Jobs and Steve Wozniak in 1978. At first only a few people could afford them, but today personal computers are found in schools, offices and homes all over the world.

Who was Mr Babbage?

In 1834, the British mathematician Charles Babbage invented the first mechanical computer that could be programmed, but he did not have the money or technology to build it. His machine was finally made in 1991 – and it worked!

How do computers work?

All computers change the information they handle into numbers, which are stored as electrical signals. In modern computers these signals are either 'on', which stands for 1, or 'off', which stands for 0. All numbers, letters and pictures are turned into a sequence of 1s and 0s (called 'binary code'). A computer does rapid calculations using these numbers, which are then changed into words and pictures that you can understand.

Can robots see?

The first industrial robot – a computer-controlled machine that carries out tasks – was made in the United States in 1962. In 1980, the first robot that could 'see' using electronic eyes was developed in America. Today, some robots have laser vision systems and can both see and hear.

Do computers have disks?

The information used to run computer programs is usually stored as electrical pulses on magnetic disks. Plastic 'floppy disks' were created by the IBM company in 1970. In 1983, compact disks (CDs), plastic-coated metal disks read by laser, went on sale. CDs used by computers can store vast amounts of information.

What is virtual reality?

The computer inside a virtual reality headset creates scenes and sounds that seem real to the wearer. This system was pioneered by Ivan Sutherland in 1965 but was not fully developed until the 1990s. Virtual reality headsets are great for games and for learning different skills.

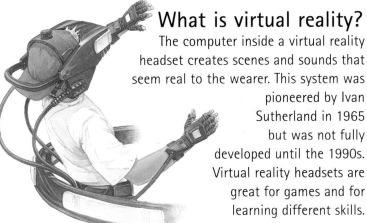

What is the Net?

Computers anywhere in the world can be linked via a telephone line and a gadget called a modem. This network, called the Internet or Net for short, is used by over 40 million people. The Internet was first developed in the late 1960s by the US government as a safe way to communicate in wartime.

Communications

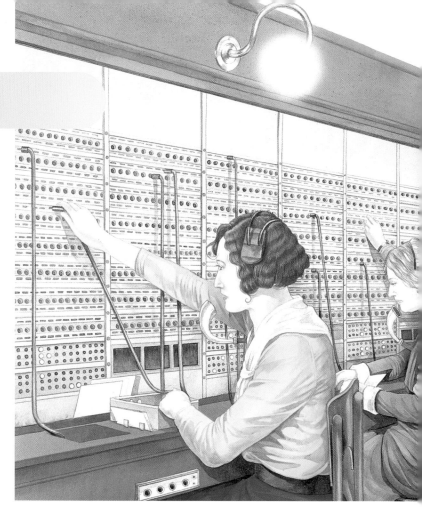

Before the printing press was invented in the 1450s, people could only swap information by word of mouth or by writing letters. Today we use books, newspapers, radio, television, telephone and e-mail to spread news and views.

Who first recorded sound?

In 1877, the famous American inventor Thomas Edison built a machine to record sound. The sounds were stored as patterns of indented lines on a tin-foil cylinder. The first words to be recorded clearly were 'Mary had a little lamb'.

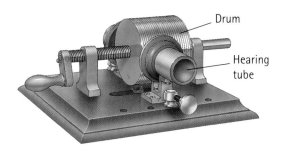

Drum

Hearing tube

Who rang the bell?

In 1875, the Scottish-American inventor Alexander Graham Bell discovered a way to send the human voice along wires. A year later he built the first working telephone and within months hundreds of telephone bells were ringing all over America.

Can glass fibres 'talk'?

Optical fibres are strands of glass twisted into a cable that can transmit light. In 1976, Charles Kao and George Hockham had the idea of using them to carry telephone calls at the speed of light. The first optical fibre telephone link was set up in America in 1977.

Who invented the radio?

The Italian Guglielmo Marconi built the first proper radio set that sent messages using radio waves in 1895. His machine produced radio waves by making a strong electric spark. The system was known as the wireless because the signals were sent through the air, not along a wire. Marconi sent the first signal across the Atlantic in 1901, and public radio broadcasts began about 20 years later.

Who said 'number please'?

The first telephone exchange set up in America in 1878 was manual, with just 21 customers. An operator answered your call, took the number you wanted and plugged in your line to complete the electrical circuit and connect your call.

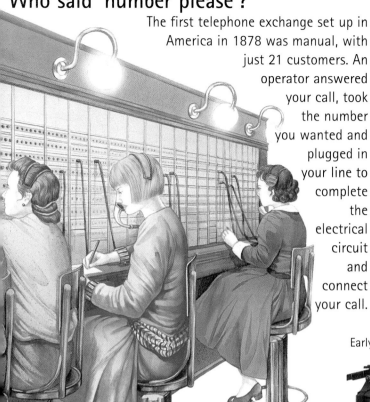

The Morse Code

a ●▬	s ●●●
b ▬●●●	t ▬
c ▬●▬●	u ●●▬
d ▬●●	v ●●●▬
e ●	w ●▬▬
f ●●▬●	x ▬●●▬
g ▬▬●	y ▬●▬▬
h ●●●●	z ▬▬●●
i ●●	0 ●▬▬▬▬▬
j ●▬▬▬	1 ●●▬▬▬▬
k ▬●▬	2 ●●●▬▬▬
l ●▬●●	3 ●●●●▬▬
m ▬▬	4 ●●●●●▬
n ▬●	5 ▬●●●●
o ▬▬▬	6 ▬▬●●●
p ●▬▬●	7 ▬▬▬●●
q ▬▬●▬	8 ▬▬▬▬●
r ●▬●	9 ▬▬▬▬▬

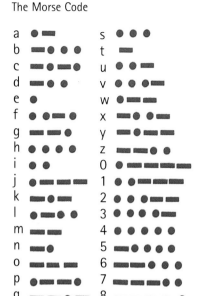

Early telegraph machine

When did phones go mobile?

In the early 1980s, computers allowed the telephone to lose its wires and go mobile. A system of low-powered radio stations link the moving telephone to a computer network that keeps track of the caller.

What is Morse Code?

Before the telephone was invented people sent messages by telegraph. This used a coded series of short and long electrical signals – dots and dashes. It was invented by the American Samuel Morse.

How do telephone calls travel round the world?

Communication satellites orbiting the Earth pick up signals and send them on to a receiver thousands of kilometres away. *Telstar*, the first one, went into orbit in 1962. It could relay 12 telephone calls or one television channel. Satellites today carry thousands of calls and several channels at once.

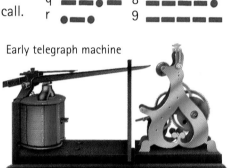

145

On Film

Before cameras were developed people could only record images by drawing or painting them. Photography was invented in the early 1800s. At first it was a slow process and all pictures were in black and white. Now we have film and video cameras to record people and places all over the world.

Who first said 'Smile, please'?

The Frenchman Joseph Niépce took the first permanent photograph in about 1827. It took eight hours for the photo of a view to develop on a thin metal plate. In the late 1800s, taking photos was such a lengthy business that people needed a back rest to help them sit still!

What is a Polaroid®?

The Polaroid® camera, invented by the American Edwin Land in 1947, produces 'instant' photos. It uses slim plastic envelopes instead of a roll of film. Inside is a sheet of film and a packet of processing chemicals, which burst as the photo is ejected. The picture develops in about 60 seconds.

Did early cameras use rolls of film?

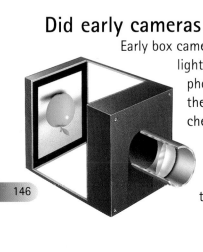

Early box cameras used a lens to focus the light rays on to a metal or glass photographic plate at the back of the camera. The light changed the chemicals on the plate and the picture developed in a few minutes. Rolls of film were first introduced in 1888 by the American George Eastman.

When did movie stars first talk?

Early movies were silent and actors had to be very good mime artists. Words came up on the screen to explain the action and an organist played mood music to liven up the film. The first full-length movie with sound was *The Jazz Singer*, shown in the United States in 1927. It was so popular that silent movies soon lost their appeal and 'talkies', talking pictures, took over.

Who invented television?

The Scottish inventor John Logie Baird first demonstrated the television in public in 1926. His original machine was made from an old box, knitting needles, a cake tin and a bicycle lamp! The first picture of a human face was a blurry image of 15-year-old William Taynton.

Rotating disc

Baird's television, 1930

Baird's camera had a mechanical scanner with a rotating disc. This was soon replaced by the electronic scanner developed by the American-Russian Vladimir Zworykin in 1923.

How do colour television cameras work?

The first colour televisions went on sale in the 1950s. Colour television cameras split the light from the scene being filmed into three images — one red, one green and one blue. The light from each image is turned into an electrical signal which is recorded with the sound signal on film or tape. A colour television converts these signals back into the coloured picture.

Quick-fire Quiz

1. When was the first 'talkie' shown?
a) 1917
b) 1927
c) 1937

2. Who invented television?
a) Thomas Edison
b) George Eastman
c) John Logie Baird

3. What did Edwin Land invent?
a) Polaroid® camera
b) Colour television
c) Movies

4. Who was the first photographer?
a) Louis Lumière
b) Auguste Lumière
c) Joseph Niépce

Who made the first movie?

The American Thomas Edison was the first person to film moving pictures, but the French brothers Auguste and Louis Lumière were the first to show a 'movie' to an audience. The brothers made 10 films in 1895 and built a machine to show them on screen to audiences in Paris clubs and cafés.

When did home videos arrive?

Videotape was invented in 1956 and the first camcorder, or video camera-recorder was developed in the 1960s. Modern lightweight camcorders went on sale in the 1980s. A camcorder uses magnetic tapes instead of photographic film to record the images and sound.

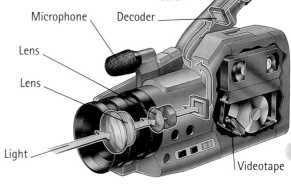

Lens

Microphone   Decoder

Lens

Lens

Light

Videotape

147

Travel on Land

Prehistoric people had to walk everywhere, carrying their goods or dragging them on sledges. By 3000 BC, people had developed wheeled vehicles pulled by animals. In the late 1800s, the invention of the steam engine and petrol engine changed land travel completely.

What is a TGV?

The French TGV, *Train à Grande Vitesse*, first went into service in 1981. These speedy electric trains can travel at over 300 kilometres an hour on special tracks. The first electric train was demonstrated at an exhibition in Germany in 1879.

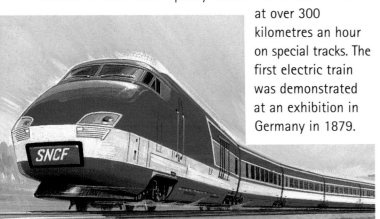

Did cars run on steam?

The first cars ran on steam, but they were noisy and often broke down. Early cars were not allowed to travel faster than walking pace and in some countries a man with a red flag had to walk in front to warn people they were coming!

Who invented the wheel?

The wheel was invented about 5,500 years ago in the Middle East. It was laid on its side and used to make pottery. About 300 years later, the Sumerians living in the same region had turned wheels upright and were using them on horse-drawn chariots. The first wheels were solid, made from three planks of wood pegged together and cut to shape. The plank wheel turned on a fixed axle.

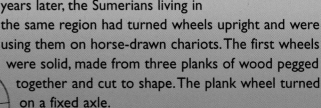

When was the bicycle invented?

The bicycle was invented in the 1790s in France, but you moved by pushing your feet along the ground! A German, Baron von Drais, made a bike with a steerable front wheel in 1817. The first bike with pedals and cranks to turn the back wheel was designed by the Scotsman Kirkpatrick Macmillan in 1839.

Can the Sun power cars?

Engineers are experimenting with a new form of energy to power car engines – energy from the Sun. Several prototypes run on solar-powered batteries. A few of these solar cars have reached speeds of 140 kilometres an hour in races across Australia.

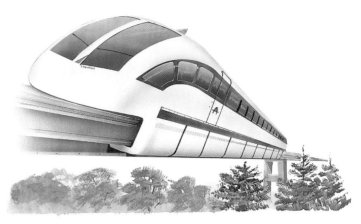

How do trains hover?

'Maglevs', or magnetic levitation trains, hover above the track supported by magnetic fields. The trains, driven by linear motors with no moving parts, can reach speeds of up to 700 kilometres an hour. These trains were pioneered in Germany and Japan in the 1980s.

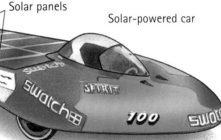

Solar panels

Solar-powered car

Who was Mr Benz?

In 1885, the German engineer Karl Benz built the first vehicle to be powered by a petrol engine. The first true four-wheeled car was developed in 1886 by another German, Gottlieb Daimler.

Which train was a winner?

In 1829, Englishman George Stevenson and his son Robert entered a contest to find the fastest steam train. Their winning engine, the *Rocket*, could pull a train at 46 kilometres an hour – twice as fast as their rivals. The first steam locomotive was developed by the English engineer Richard Trevithick in 1803.

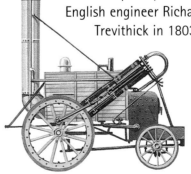

What was a Tin Lizzie?

Hand-built early cars were too expensive for ordinary people. But in 1908, in America, Henry Ford had the idea of mass-producing cars on his other invention –

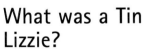

the assembly line. In the next 20 years, he sold 15 million 'Model T' cars, also known as Tin Lizzies.

Quick-fire Quiz

1. What was a Tin Lizzie?
a) A train
b) A car
c) A bicycle

2. Who built the first petrol-powered vehicle?
a) Daimler
b) Benz
c) Ford

3. Who built the first steam train?
a) George Stevenson
b) Henry Ford
c) Richard Trevithick

4. How fast could the *Rocket* travel?
a) 56 km/h
b) 46 km/h
c) 36 km/h

On the Sea

Early people travelled over water using rafts and dug-out canoes. About 5,000 years ago the Sumerians and Egyptians built ships with sails and oars. In the 1800s steam engines took over from sails and steel replaced wood. A hundred years later, ships with petrol engines took to the waves.

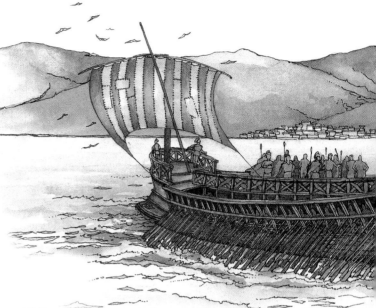

What was a trireme?

Triremes were fast galleys powered by three rows of oarsmen on each side. The Greeks first built triremes in about 650 BC. Later triremes were up to 40 metres long with a pointed ram at the front to smash into enemy ships.

When were paddle steamers first used?

The Frenchman Jouffroy d'Abbans built the first working steamboat in 1783. Within 20 years paddle steamers were being used to ferry people and goods up and down rivers and across the sea.

How did sailors find their way?

In the mid-1700s, two British inventions helped sailors fix their position at sea. The sextant, invented by John Campbell, determined latitude by measuring the angle of the Sun or stars above the horizon. John Harrison's chronometer – a kind of clock – helped to measure longitude.

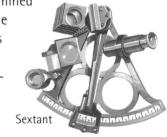

Sextant

How do divers swim underwater?

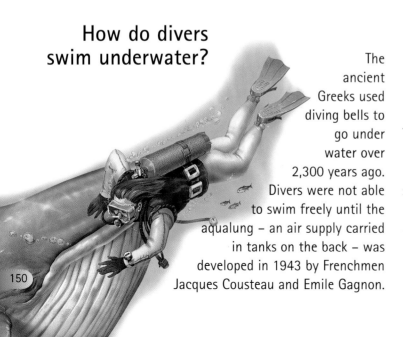

The ancient Greeks used diving bells to go under water over 2,300 years ago. Divers were not able to swim freely until the aqualung – an air supply carried in tanks on the back – was developed in 1943 by Frenchmen Jacques Cousteau and Emile Gagnon.

Why were clippers fast?

The super-fast clipper of the mid-1800s had a new shape of hull and a combination of square and triangular sails with which it could catch and use the slightest breeze. Clippers could maintain speeds of 37 kilometres an hour.

Quick-fire Quiz

1. When was the first steamboat trip?
a) 1683
b) 1783
c) 1883

2. Who designed the hovercraft?
a) Campbell
b) Cockerel
c) Gagnon

3. What was the Turtle?
a) A steamship
b) An aircraft carrier
c) A submarine

4. Who first built triremes?
a) Romans
b) Egyptians
c) Greeks

When were submarines invented?

In 1620, the Dutchman Cornelius Drebbel's wooden submarine, rowed by 12 oarsmen, travelled several kilometres up the River Thames in London, England. The *Turtle*, the first submarine that could rise and sink, was designed by the American David Bushnell in 1776. It was used in the American War of Independence.

The *Turtle*

What craft floats on air?

Hovercraft can skim over land or water on a cushion of air blown down by fans and trapped inside a flexible rubber skirt. The hovercraft was designed by the British engineer Christopher Cockerel in the 1950s and made its first test run in 1959.

How do jet aircraft land on ships?

The first carrier for jet aircraft, *USS Forrestal*, was completed in 1955. Aircraft can take off and land on the deck in mid-ocean. During take-off the aircraft is propelled forward by a device called a 'catapult'. When it lands, the aircraft is slowed down by huge 'arrester' wires stretched across the deck.

151

By Air

Over 2,000 years ago the Chinese flew war kites to fire-bomb their enemies. Air transport did not begin until the 1780s, when hot-air balloons took to the skies. Just over 100 years later, powered flight got off to a bumpy start.

When was the first flight?

The first flight was made in a hot-air balloon on 21 November 1783 by François de Rozier and the Marquis d'Arlandes. The balloon, made by the French Montgolfier brothers, had a basket for passengers slung beneath the huge paper balloon.

How do hang-gliders fly?

Hang-gliders depend on the wind and rising warm air to fly. In 1853, British engineer George Cayley was the first to design a suitably shaped wing. Nearly 100 years later, in the 1940s, the American Francis Rogallo developed a triangular-shaped kite that gave rise to modern hang-gliders.

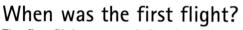

Who was the first hang-glider?

Otto Lilienthal, a German engineer, designed and flew over 15 different hang-gliders. He made the first flight in which the pilot controlled the machine. Lilienthal died in 1896 when his hang-glider crashed.

Who were the Wright brothers?

The American brothers Orville and Wilbur Wright had the idea of fitting a petrol engine and propeller to their glider. On 17 December 1903, Orville made the world's first powered flight. *Flyer 1* flew for 12 seconds and covered 37 metres – less than the length of a jumbo jet!

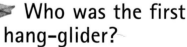

How do helicopters rise up vertically?

Helicopters have one or two large rotors made up of long, thin wings. When the rotors spin round, they lift the aircraft and drive it along. Helicopters can fly forwards, backwards and sideways. The first single-blade helicopter was built by Russian-American Sikorsky in 1939.

Can aeroplanes land by themselves?

Modern jet liners are controlled from a hi-tech flight deck. They even have computer-controlled autopilot systems to land planes in bad weather when the pilot cannot see the runway clearly. The first autopilot landing of a scheduled airliner was in 1965 at Heathrow Airport, England.

What were zeppelins?

Zeppelins, named after their German inventor Ferdinand von Zeppelin, were giant airships up to 240 metres in length. They were powered by petrol engines and a propeller, and filled with hydrogen gas which is lighter than air but very flammable. The first zeppelin flight was in 1900.

Jet power – when and where?

Gloster
E28/39 jet

In the 1930s, both Britain and Germany were working on a new form of power for aircraft – the jet engine. The British engineer Frank Whittle came up with the idea in 1929, and prototypes were built by Whittle in Britain and by Hans von Ohain in Germany. The first jet aircraft, built by the German Ernst Heinkel, took to the air in 1939. Two years later, Whittle's engine powered the Gloster E28/39 jet. Jet engines allow planes to travel much faster – some military jets can zoom along at 3,200 kilometres an hour!

Are helicopters really 500 years old?

The Italian artist and inventor Leonardo da Vinci sketched a simple helicopter (see above) over 500 years ago, but it was never built. The French inventor Paul Cornu built the first helicopter in 1907 – it rose to a height of 30 centimetres and hovered there for 20 seconds. Cornu's helicopter was very difficult to control, and it was not until the 1930s that helicopters became a practical means of flying.

Quick-fire Quiz

1. Name the Wright brothers' first plane:
a) Gloster
b) Flyer 1
c) Orville

2. Who was the first hang-glider pilot?
a) Zeppelin
b) Whittle
c) Lilienthal

3. Which gas was used in zeppelins?
a) Oxygen
b) Air
c) Hydrogen

4. Who sketched the first helicopter?
a) George Cayley
b) Montgolfier brothers
c) Leonardo da Vinci

Into Space

In the early 1950s, the United States and Soviet Union began the space race. In 1957 the Russians launched the first satellite, *Sputnik I*. Four years later, the Russian cosmonaut Yuri Gagarin blasted into orbit in *Vostock I*. His historic trip round the world lasted for under 2 hours, but manned space flight was launched.

Who first saw stars?

In 1609, the Italian scientist Galileo was the first person to look at the stars through a telescope. His studies led him to suggest that the Earth moved round the Sun and was not at the centre of the Universe as people then thought.

Why do telescopes detect radio waves?

Stars and other objects in space give out radio waves as well as light. Radio telescopes have huge dish-shaped antennae to pick up these radio waves. Radio telescopes have discovered exploding galaxies, radiation from distant galaxies and spinning neutron stars called pulsars.

Is there life on other planets?

The other planets in our Solar System are probably not able to support life, but scientists are looking further afield. In 1974, astronomers beamed a radio message out into space from a huge radio telescope in Puerto Rico. They aimed it at a dense star cluster, M13, over 25,000 light years away. The message is travelling at the speed of light so we will have to wait 50,000 years for a reply!

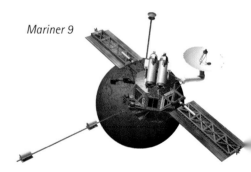

Mariner 9

What is a space probe?

Space probes are unmanned spacecraft that travel into space. Several have been sent to other planets in the Solar System. *Mariner 9*, launched in 1971, visited Mars. *Mariner 10*, launched in 1973, was the first probe to visit two planets. It flew by Venus and visited Mercury three times, where it found that the daytime temperatures were hot enough to melt lead.

Who was the first man on the Moon?

The American Neil Armstrong was the first man to set foot on the Moon in July 1969. He and fellow astronaut Edwin 'Buzz' Aldrin put up the American flag and a plaque saying 'We come in peace for all mankind'.

When did people first walk in space?

In 1965, the Russian Aleksei Leonov made the first space walk, but he had to remain attached to the spacecraft. In the early 1980s, scientists developed the MMU (manned manoeuvring unit), which let astronauts walk freely in space.

Quick-fire Quiz

1. Who was the first on the Moon?
   a) Edwin Aldrin
   b) Yuri Gagarin
   c) Neil Armstrong

2. When did the shuttle first 'fly'?
   a) 1971
   b) 1981
   c) 1991

3. What was *Salyut I*?
   a) A rocket
   b) A space probe
   c) A space station

4. What was the first satellite called?
   a) *Mir*
   b) *Sputnik I*
   c) *Challenger*

What is a shuttle?

Early spacecraft used rocket power to blast them into space. Then the Americans came up with the idea of building a re-usable spacecraft. The shuttle still needs rocket power to take off, but it lands like an aircraft and so can be re-used. In 1981, the first space shuttle, *Columbia*, took off.

What is a space station?

Space stations are large spacecraft that spend several years orbiting the Earth. The first space station was the Russian *Salyut I*, which was launched in 1971. Modern space stations like the Russian *Mir* use solar panels to power the station while it is in orbit. The crew can stay up in space for many months carrying out scientific experiments and repairing equipment.

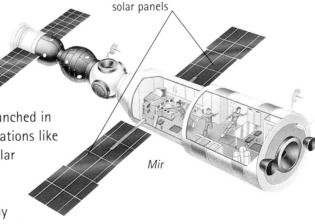

solar panels

Mir

Timeline

Hundreds of inventions and discoveries have marked human progress from the Stone Age to the Space Age. Some happened by accident, others took people years to perfect. Here are a few important milestones.

20000 BC to 2000 BC

c.20000 BC Bone needles used

c.8000 BC First permanent houses built

4000–3000 BC Earliest known writing (cuneiform) (Sumeria)

3500 BC Simple ploughs pulled by people (Sumeria)

3200 BC About 300 years after the potter's wheel was invented, people made simple wheeled vehicles (Sumeria)

3000 BC Simple glass beads made (Egypt)

c.2800 BC Stonehenge built in England; first step pyramids built in Egypt

2350 BC First lavatories with pedestals (Mesopotamia)

1900 BC to 0

c.1900 BC Metal workers began extracting iron from its ore; steel was made c.1200 BC

1000–700 First shadow clocks (Egypt); by 700 BC divided sundial was in use

c.690 BC First bridges (aqueducts) used to carry water (Assyria)

c.620 BC First coins made from electrum in Lydia (Asia Minor)

c.450 BC Decimal abacus c.450 BC; early stick and dust tray abacus (Mesopotamia c.2500 BC)

c.85 BC First water-powered mills used to grind flour (Greece)

AD 1 to 1400

105 Tsai Lun made paper from pulp (China)

600 Chess developed (India or China)

c.840 Camera obscura developed (China)

c.868 First printed book *Diamond Sutra* (China)

c.1000 Spinning wheel used (Asia)

c.1090 Magnetic compass invented (China, Arabia)

c.1300 First mechanical clocks with equal time periods developed (Europe)

c.1300 Astrolabe adapted for sea navigation (Arabia)

1401 to 1700

c.1440 Johannes Gutenberg developed printing press with movable type (Germany); first book printed c.1450

c.1590 Janssen made compound microscope (Netherlands)

c.1592 Galileo made first thermometer (Italy)

1608 Hans Lippershey made working telescope (Netherlands)

1609 Galileo first person to look at stars (Italy)

c. 1620 Drebble built first submarine (England)

c. 1642 Pascal built calculating machine (France)

c.1683 Antonie van Leeuwenhoek made first high-power (x 200) microscope (Netherlands)

1701 to 1800

1712 Newcomen built steam-powered engine (England)

1714 Fahrenheit developed mercury thermometer (Germany)

1752 Franklin developed lightning conductor (USA)

1757 John Campbell built sextant (England)

1759 Harrison developed accurate chronometer (England)

1764 James Hargreaves built spinning jenny (England)

1765 Watt built condensing steam engine (Scotland)

1769 Richard Arkwright built powered spinning machine (England)

1783 Montgolfier brothers built first practical hot-air balloon (France)

1783 Jouffroy D'Abbans built first steam boat (France)

1785 Cartwright built power loom (England)

1801 to 1900

1803 Richard Trevethick built steam train (England)

1821 Michael Faraday made first electric motor (England)

c.1827 First photograph taken by Niépce (France)

1829 Stevenson's steam train *Rocket* was built (England)

1829 Sewing machine built by Thimonnier (France)

1837 Telegraph developed by Morse (USA) and Cooke and Wheatstone (England)

1839 First practical bicycle built by Kirkpatrick Macmillan (Scotland)

1852 Henri Gifford built first working (steam-powered) airship (France)

1853 George Cayley pioneered glider technology (England)

1856 Henry Bessemer invented cheap steel-making process (England)

1865 Lister first used antiseptics (England)

1867 Joseph Monier developed wire-reinforced concrete (France)

1873 C. L. Sholes made first practical commercial typewriter (USA) (went on sale in 1874)

1875 Scot Alexander Graham Bell invented telephone (USA)

1877 Thomas Edison developed the phonograph (USA)

1878/9 Swan (England) and Edison (USA) made electric light bulb

1882 First power station opened by Edison (USA)

1882 Henry Seely built first practical electric iron (USA)

1884 Gottlieb Daimler made first light-weight petrol engines (Germany)

1885 Karl Benz made first petrol-driven motor car (Germany)

1893 W. Judson made the first slide fastener (USA)

1895 Wilhelm Röntgen discovered X-rays (Germany)

1895 Marconi invented radio communication (Italy)

1895 Auguste and Louis Lumière first showed a 'movie' to an audience (France)

1901 to 2000

1903 Wright brothers flew first powered aircraft (USA)

1907 First helicopter built by Paul Cornu (France)

1925 John Logie Baird invented television and demonstrated it in 1926 (Scotland)

1929 Whittle patented idea of the jet engine (England)

1933 Polythene discovered at ICI (England)

1935 Wallace Carothers made nylon (USA)

1936 Focke made first practical helicopter (Germany)

1942 Enrico Fermi built first nuclear reactor (USA)

1945 Mauchly and Eckert developed first proper computer (USA)

1947 Edwin Land invented polaroid camera (USA)

1948 First atomic clock built (USA)

1953 DNA double-helix discovered by F. Crick (England), J Watson (USA) and M. Wilkins (England)

1955 Cockerel invented hovercraft (England)

1957 First artificial Earth satellite went into orbit (USSR)

1959 Integrated circuit (silicon chip) developed (USA)

1960 T. Maiman developed laser (USA)

1961 First manned space flight (Russia)

1964 Computer mouse invented by Engelhart (USA)

1967 First heart transplant by C. Barnard (South Africa)

1969 First manned moon landing (USA)

1970 Floppy disk developed by IBM (USA)

1971 Microprocessor patented by Intel (USA)

1978 Successful PC developed by Jobs and Wozniak (USA)

1979 Compact disk developed by Sony and Philips

1981 Space shuttle developed (USA)

1983 Satellite TV developed (USA)

1984 Genetic fingerprinting developed (Britain)

1989 Game Boy™ launched by Nintendo (Japan)

c1992 Virtual reality helmets devised (USA)

1992 First map of human chromosome (France, Britain, USA)

1994 Longest undersea tunnel, 50km-long Channel Tunnel opens (Britain, France)

1995 First DNA database set up (Britain)

1997 First successful clone of a mammal (Britain)

c.1997 Sikorsky developed robotic helicopter (USA)

1997 Biorobotics pioneered by Shimoyama's team (Japan)

Index

159

Index

Quick-fire Quiz
ANSWERS

Page 9 Looking at the Sky
1. b   2. c   3. b   4. b

Page 11 Seeing Stars
1. b   2. c   3. b   4. b

Page 12 Great Balls of Gas
1. b   2. b   3. c   4. c

Page 15 Galaxies
1. c   2. b   3. c   4. a

Page 17 The Solar System
1. b   2. c   3. b   4. c

Page 18 Our Star the Sun
1. b   2. c   3. b   4. c

Page 21 The Planets
1. b   2. c   3. b   4. b

Page 23 Mercury
1. b   2. c   3. b   4. a

Page 25 Venus
1. c   2. b   3. c   4. a

Page 27 Earth
1. b   2. b   3. c   4. a

Page 29 The Moon
1. c   2. b   3. c   4. b

Page 31 Mars
1. c   2. b   3. a   4. c

Page 33 Jupiter
1. c   2. a   3. c   4. b

Page 35 Saturn
1. c   2. b   3. b   4. a

Page 37 Uranus
1. c   2. c   3. b   4. c

Page 39 Neptune and Pluto
1. b   2. c   3. b   4. c

Page 41 Asteroids
1. c   2. b   3. c   4. a

Page 43 Comets
1. b   2. b   3. a   4. c

Page 47 Digging up the Facts
1. b   2. c   3. c   4. b

Page 49 Colour and Camouflage
1. b   2. a   3. b   4. a

Page 51 Dinosaur Giants
1. c   2. a   3. a   4. c

Page 53 Small Dinosaurs
1. c   2. c   3. a   4. b

Page 55 Dinosaur Babies
1. b   2. a   3. c   4. b

Page 57 Communication
1. a   2. a   3. c   4. c

Page 59 Plant-Eaters
1. b   2. c   3. c   4. b

Page 61 Meat-Eaters
1. c   2. c   3. b   4. a

Page 63 The Fiercest Dinosaur
1. b   2. c   3. b   4. b

Page 65 Attack and Defence
1. a   2. b   3. b   4. c

Page 67 All Over the World
1. b   2. b   3. b   4. c

Page 69 Living in Herds
1. a   2. b   3. b   4. c

Page 71 Fast and Slow
1. b   2. b   3. b   4. c

Page 73 In the Sea
1. c   2. a   3. c   4. b

Page 75 In the Air
1. b   2. c   3. a   4. b

Page 77 Death of the Dinosaurs
1. c   2. a   3. b   4. b

Page 79 Timescale
1. b   2. b   3. c   4. b

Page 81 After the Dinosaurs
1. a   2. c   3. b   4. c

Page 85 The First Peoples
1. c   2. a   3. b   4. a

Page 87 River Valley Civilizations
1. b   2. a   3. c   4. c

Page 89 Ancient Egypt
1. b   2. b   3. c   4. b

Page 91 Priests and Mummies
1. b   2. a   3. b   4. c

Page 93 Pyramids and Tombs
1. b   2. a   3. c   4. b

Page 95 Crete and Mycenae
1. c   2. b   3. c   4. a

Page 97 Babylon
1. b   2. a   3. a   4. c

Page 99 Assyrians and Hittites
1. a   2. c   3. b   4. c

Page 101 Ancient Sea Traders
1. a   2. b   3. b   4. c

Page 103 Ancient Greece
1. c   2. b   3. b   4. a

Page 105 Greek Life
1. b   2. a   3. c   4. a

Page 107 The Persians
1. a   2. b   3. c   4. c

Page 109 Ancient China
1. b   2. c   3. b   4. a

Page 111 The Celts
1. b   2. c   3. a   4. c

Page 113 Life in Ancient Rome
1. a   2. b   3. c   4. b

Page 115 The Roman Empire
1. b   2. a   3. c   4. c

Page 117 The Mayan Empire
1. b   2. c   3. a   4. a

Page 123 Writing and Printing
1. a   2. c   3. c   4. b

Page 125 Medicine
1. c   2. b   3. a   4. c

Page 127 Buildings
1. c   2. b   3. b   4. c

Page 129 Food and Agriculture
1. b   2. c   3. a   4. b

Page 131 At Home
1. c   2. b   3. a   4. b

Page 133 Clothes and Fabric
1. c   2. c   3. c   4. a

Page 135 Useful Materials
1. b   2. c   3. b   4. a

Page 137 Toys and Games
1. b   2. a   3. b   4. c

Page 139 Energy
1. b   2. c   3. a   4. c

Page 141 Calculations
1. b   2. c   3. b   4. b

Page 143 Computers
1. b   2. c   3. a   4. c

Page 145 Communication
1. b   2. c   3. b   4. b

Page 147 On Film
1. b   2. c   3. a   4. c

Page 149 Travel on Land
1. b   2. b   3. c   4. b

Page 151 On the Sea
1. b   2. b   3. c   4. c

Page 153 By Air
1. b   2. c   3. c   4. c

Page 155 Into Space
1. c   2. b   3. c   4. b